GENESIS to REVELATION
1 AND 2 KINGS
1 AND 2 CHRONICLES

CHARLES R. BRITT

GENESIS to REVELATION
1 AND 2 KINGS
1 AND 2 CHRONICLES

CHARLES R. BRITT

GENESIS TO REVELATION SERIES:
1 AND 2 KINGS
1 AND 2 CHRONICLES
PARTICIPANT

Copyright © 1982 by Graded Press
Revised Edition Copyright ©1997 by Abingdon Press
Updated and Revised Edition Copyright © 2018 by Abingdon Press
All rights reserved.

No part of this work may be reproduced or transmitted in any form or by any means, electronic or mechanical, including photocopying and recording, or by any information or retrieval system, except as may be expressly permitted in the 1976 Copyright Act or in writing from the publisher. Requests for permission should be addressed in writing to Permissions, The United Methodist Publishing House, 2222 Rosa L. Parks Blvd., Nashville, TN 37228 or e-mailed to permissions@umpublishing.org.

All Scripture quotations, unless otherwise indicated, are taken from the Holy Bible, New International Version®, NIV®. Copyright ©1973, 1978, 1984, 2011 by Biblica, Inc.™ Used by permission of Zondervan. All rights reserved worldwide. www.zondervan.com The "NIV" and "New International Version" are trademarks registered in the United States Patent and Trademark Office by Biblica, Inc.™

Scripture quotations marked (CEV) are from the Contemporary English Version Copyright © 1991, 1992, 1995 by American Bible Society, Used by Permission.

Scripture quotations marked (CEB) are from the Common English Bible, copyright 2011. Used by permission. All rights reserved.

ISBN 9781501855566
Manufactured in the United States of America

18 19 20 21 22 23 24 25 26 27—10 9 8 7 6 5 4 3 2 1

ABINGDON PRESS
Nashville

TABLE OF CONTENTS

1. Solomon's Accomplishments (1 Kings 1–9) 6
2. The End of Solomon's Reign (1 Kings 10–20) 15
3. Elijah and Elisha (1 Kings 21–2 Kings 8) 25
4. The Decline of Israel (2 Kings 9–17) 32
5. The Kingdom of Judah (2 Kings 18–25) 39
6. Genealogies (1 Chronicles 1–8) 49
7. David, the Great King (1 Chronicles 9–14) 57
8. The Ark of the Covenant (1 Chronicles 15–21) 64
9. The Temple and Its Rituals (1 Chronicles 22–29) 72
10. The Reign of Solomon (2 Chronicles 1–9) 79
11. The Kingdom Is Divided (2 Chronicles 10–16) 86
12. Judah's Kings (2 Chronicles 17–26) 94
13. Hezekiah and Josiah (2 Chronicles 27–36) 102

Map: The Kingdoms of Israel and Judah 111

The kingdom was now firmly established in Solomon's hands.
(2:46)

1

SOLOMON'S ACCOMPLISH-MENTS
1 Kings 1–9

DIMENSION ONE: WHAT DOES THE BIBLE SAY?

Answer these questions by reading 1 Kings 1

1. What does Bathsheba want for Solomon? (1:13)

2. Who challenges this ambition? (1:5)

3. What things may have spoiled Adonijah? (1:6)

4. How does David ensure Solomon's right to the throne? (1:32-40)

5. Why does Adonijah hold onto the horns of the altar? (1:50-51)

SOLOMON'S ACCOMPLISHMENTS

Answer these questions by reading 1 Kings 2

6. How does David feel about dying? (2:2)

7. What does David tell Solomon to do? (2:5-9)

8. How many years does David reign as king? (2:11)

Answer these questions by reading 1 Kings 3

9. What two things does Solomon do that David did not do? (3:3)

10. What gift does Solomon ask from God? (3:9)

11. How does God respond to Solomon's request? (3:10)

12. How does Solomon show his wisdom? (3:16-28)

Answer these questions by reading 1 Kings 6-7

13. What materials are used in building the temple? (6:31-36)

14. How many years are spent building the temple? (6:38)

15. How long does Solomon work on his palace? (7:1)

16. What does Huram do for King Solomon? (7:13-14)

Answer these questions by reading 1 Kings 8

17. Where is the ark of the covenant placed in the temple? (8:6)

18. What objects are in the ark? (8:9)

19. How do the priests know God is in the temple? (8:10-11)

20. What does Solomon ask God to do when the people pray? (8:30)

21. Does Solomon believe that all people sin? (8:46)

Answer these questions by reading 1 Kings 9

22. What does God want Solomon to do? (9:4)

23. Where does Solomon keep his fleet of ships? (9:26)

SOLOMON'S ACCOMPLISHMENTS

DIMENSION TWO: WHAT DOES THE BIBLE MEAN?

These nine chapters are important because they record the end of David's reign and Solomon's accession to the throne. Solomon's two chief accomplishments—building the temple and constructing his great palace—are recorded in these chapters.

In 1 Kings 1–9, the rule of the house of David over Israel is seen as fulfilling God's desire for the chosen people. Also, all history is interpreted according to what is called the Deuteronomic pattern: Life for a people is good when the rulers and people obey God and bad for them when they disobey God.

■ **1 Kings 1:14.** The people in the ancient Near East felt there was a close connection between their king's sexual vigor and the strength and health of their nation. David's impotence is much more than the record of an old man's declining years. It has political implications and is probably a major force leading to the struggle for the throne. If David is impotent, he is unfit to be king. A change in authority is due.

■ **1 Kings 1:5-58.** Three family members are involved in the power struggle: Adonijah, the oldest surviving son of David; Bathsheba, who became David's wife following acts of adultery and murder (2 Samuel 11); and Bathsheba's son, Solomon. Bathsheba is aided by Nathan, the prophet who rebuked David for his sin with her (2 Samuel 12).

When Adonijah's attempt at kingship fails, he flees to the altar of God for protection. The four horns of the altar, symbols of strength and vitality, were places where persons, fearing for their lives, could take hold and find safety (see also 1 Kings 2:28; Exodus 21:13-14; 27:2).

■ **1 Kings 2:1-12.** David's legacy to Solomon includes the throne, moral advice, and practical but bloodthirsty instructions. Solomon is to be faithful to God in terms of ritual and morality ("decrees and commands," v. 3). David tells him to put two of his old opponents, Joab and Shimei, to death. He is charged to deal generously with the men who supported David during Absalom's revolt (2 Samuel 15).

■ **1 Kings 2:13-25.** In 2:12, we read that Solomon's kingdom is firmly established, but apparently he still feels threatened by Adonijah. When Adonijah asks for Abishag as his wife, Solomon sees this request as another bid for the throne.

■ **1 Kings 2:26-46.** David's deathbed advice is carried out by Solomon.

■ **1 Kings 3:1-28.** These "high places" (v. 2) are pagan Canaanite shrines that have been taken over for the worship of Yahweh. The Deuteronomic view of religion and history sees these shrines as unworthy. Solomon's marriages to non-Hebrew wives are also seen as a moral and spiritual threat to Solomon's wholehearted allegiance (see 1 Kings 11:1-13).

Solomon's prayer for wisdom to govern the people elicits a response from God that calls to mind the Spirit of Matthew 6:33. Solomon has chosen to ask for something that God delights to give.

■ **1 Kings 4:1–5:18.** The reign of Solomon is remembered as a time of great national prosperity and expansion. Verses 20 and 25 are grateful summaries of the blessings of the era.

■ **1 Kings 4:29-34.** The scope of Solomon's wisdom is indicated by noting the range of his intellectual interests. Part of our association of Solomon with the book of Proverbs begins here.

■ **1 Kings 5–7.** Solomon chooses Mount Moriah, a hill just north of Jerusalem, as the site for three units of buildings: a governmental complex, his house and a house for Pharaoh's daughter, and the temple (see 2 Chronicles 3:1).

Chapter 7 gives the details of Solomon's building program. Whereas the temple construction took seven years to complete, the palace and governmental complex took thirteen years.

SOLOMON'S ACCOMPLISHMENTS

■ **1 Kings 8:1-9.** At the very center of this new and costly splendor rests the ark of the covenant. The ark is placed in the Most Holy Place. In verse 9, that little word *except* sounds as if nothing of importance is in the ark; however, that is not true. In the ark are two plain blocks of stone that are perhaps like roofing slate. On these tables of stone, carved in Hebrew, are what we know as the Ten Commandments. In Hebrew, these are known as "the Ten Words," the Decalogue. They consist of ten brief phrases, many of them only two words long. These "Ten Words" are the foundation of all Hebrew religion and the foundation of basic Christian morality (see Deuteronomy 10:1-5).

■ **1 Kings 8:10-11.** In the books of Exodus, Leviticus, and Numbers, a cloud is evidence of God's presence with the Hebrew people. The cloud is proof of God's guidance while they journey, just as the stone tablets are evidence of God's concern for the quality of the Israelites' life. The Ten Words are God's law. The cloud is God's presence. Now that the temple is to be the place where Israel meets God, the cloud is witness to the Lord's presence.

■ **1 Kings 8:14-66.** This section is an Old Testament high priestly prayer. Nothing like it appears again in the Scripture until we come to the New Testament. There, in John 17, Jesus prays for his people.

How great is the God that Solomon addresses! God keeps the covenant with the Israelites and shows them steadfast love. The Lord chooses to have the divine name in the temple. When we remember that, for the Hebrews, a name was equivalent to the character of a person or of God, this association of God's name with the temple indicates that the character of God will be made known here and celebrated as the years go by.

■ **1 Kings 8:54-61.** How is Israel to respond to Solomon's prayer? The benediction Solomon pronounces in 8:54-61 spells out the response the Israelites are to make to the God whose people they are.

■ **1 Kings 9.** Here the historian sums up the material and human cost of the magnificence with which Solomon surrounds himself.

DIMENSION THREE: WHAT DOES THE BIBLE MEAN TO ME?

The Bible means precisely what we allow it to mean. We can treat these passages as if they were nothing more than a record of ancient, although fascinating, history. Some persons have insisted on finding here, particularly in the description of the temple, a great source of exotic symbolism for Christian faith and discipleship.

Other people have discovered in these chapters some basic themes that bear directly upon our faith, our worship, and our work as Christian disciples in the twenty-first century: (1) God's involvement in human history, (2) the value of our labor on behalf of the kingdom of God, and (3) the need of the human heart for a special place of meeting with God.

1 Kings 1–3—God's Involvement in History

God is involved in human history. The thrust of God in human history is toward freedom, independence, well-being of the community, and peace. God brought the Hebrews out of Egyptian slavery and into the Promised Land. Now God is establishing them as a nation committed to service to the Lord.

God does not use perfect persons to achieve these goals. There are no perfect persons. So, as we find God working through the imperfect David and the less-than-perfect Saul, we may continue to expect God to use imperfect persons, including each of us. When have you felt that God was using you for a particular goal?

SOLOMON'S ACCOMPLISHMENTS

When imperfect persons endeavor to be obedient and to serve God, they find that God will supply their needs. As Solomon received wisdom for his task of ruling, so may we be given wisdom, strength, and hope for our tasks in God's service.

1 Kings 5–7—The Value of Our Labor

The quality of our labor is important in the life of God's kingdom. Many varied and wonderful materials were used in building the temple. We get the feeling of value, splendor, and abundance as we read. Nothing seems to have been too good for the temple. Nothing seems to have been withheld.

We are privileged to live in the centuries after Christ and in the season of the Holy Spirit (see John 7:39). Our task includes the building of temples for the worship of God and the heralding of God's character. Because of that character, we also build schools, hospitals, refuges for battered women and children, and homes for aging persons in need of security. We turn our attention to questions of poverty and hunger, discrimination and exploitation, war and peace.

As in the building of Solomon's Temple, nothing is too valuable to be given in our labor for the kingdom. What materials of value do we have to give for this purpose? What things would we have difficulty giving up?

1 Kings 8—A Special Meeting Place

The human heart has a need for personal encounter with God. We need a specific point in time and place where God meets with us and where we feel and know that God is near.

Solomon prayed that the temple would be such a place. He prayed that there the Hebrews would experience God's grace in repentance, judgment, forgiveness, renewal, support, and continuance as the chosen ones.

We also need such places and times. This is why the church where you worship today is so greatly loved. It is why the returning hours of prayer are so rich. But because of Christ, because of the Holy Spirit, we know that God doesn't only meet us within the confines of a church or temple. All hours and all places are for the meeting of God with the people (see John 4:23). What are these places and times in your life?

This prayer of Solomon is serious worship. It is not just rejoicing in the soft and pleasurable aspects of God's dealings with the Israelites. This prayer seeks and accepts God's intensely moral impact upon human life.

Our worship and our prayer, wherever and whenever, must include confession of our sins; affirmation of God's gracious, loving character; and commitment to forsake our wrongdoing.

*Then [Solomon] rested with his ancestors. . . . And Rehoboam
his son succeeded him as king. (11:43)*

THE END OF SOLOMON'S REIGN

1 Kings 10–20

DIMENSION ONE: WHAT DOES THE BIBLE SAY?

Answer these questions by reading 1 Kings 10

1. What queen asks Solomon hard questions? (10:1)

2. What tokens of friendship do Solomon and this queen exchange? (10:10-13)

3. How do Solomon's wealth and wisdom compare to those of other kings? (10:23)

Answer these questions by reading 1 Kings 11

4. How do Solomon's wives influence him? (11:1-4)

15

5. How is Solomon's infidelity to be punished? (11:11)

6. Why does God's punishment become less severe? (11:12-13)

7. What happens as a result of God's anger? (11:14, 23, 26)

8. To what book does the writer of First Kings refer? (11:41)

9. Who succeeds Solomon? (11:43)

Answer these questions by reading 1 Kings 12–13

10. What happens after Rehoboam becomes king? (12:16-20)

11. How does Jeroboam try to gain the loyalty of the people? (12:25-33)

12. What will happen to Jeroboam? (13:34)

Answer these questions by reading 1 Kings 14–15

13. How do Judah and Israel get along? (14:30)

THE END OF SOLOMON'S REIGN

14. Why does God continue to show favor to Solomon's descendants? (15:4)

15. What sin of David continues to be remembered? (15:5)

16. Who are the next two kings over Judah? (14:31; 15:8)

17. What does Asa do? (15:11-14)

18. Who are the kings in Israel after Jeroboam? (15:25, 33; 16:8, 15, 23, 29)

Answer these questions by reading 1 Kings 16–19

19. Why is Ahab punished? (16:30-33)

20. What great prophet appears during the reign of Ahab? (17:1)

21. What does Elijah say God is going to do? (17:1)

22. 'Where does Elijah demonstrate God's supremacy over the prophets of Baal? (18:20)

23. Whom does God appoint to take Elijah's place? (19:16)

DIMENSION TWO: WHAT DOES THE BIBLE MEAN?

■ **1 Kings 10–11.** Chapters 10 and 11 complete the story of Solomon's reign. He is king over the nation inherited from his father, David. Here we have a simple, straightforward description of the glory of Solomon in wisdom, wealth, and international fame.

Historians date the death of Solomon to the year 922 BC. At this point, the history of the Hebrew people becomes confusing. The record moves us back and forth between the two kingdoms, Israel in the north and Judah in the south.

Saul had united the people into a single kingdom about 1020 BC. The United Kingdom continued for ninety-eight years, ruled by Saul, David, and then Solomon. Tragedy begins with the death of Solomon and the succession of Rehoboam. This tragedy finally plays itself out after the end of the book of Second Chronicles.

Rehoboam is a sadly misguided young king. Under his threats, the kingdom divides. One tribe, Judah, remains faithful to Rehoboam and the house of David (see 1 Kings 11:32; 12:21). The other tribes withdraw and become the Northern Kingdom, Israel. The kingdom remains divided until 722 BC, when Israel disappears as a viable political entity.

■ **1 Kings 12:1-20.** What splendid possibilities are before Rehoboam when he comes to the throne of the United Kingdom! What a great future seems possible for him and his people. He could, as heir to Solomon's wealth and power, lead the Hebrews into a golden age. Unfortunately, he lacks his father's wisdom. The golden age does not come because Rehoboam chooses to act upon some of the worst advice ever given a new ruler.

Solomon's program of taxation and forced labor has been painful. The people petition Rehoboam for relief, but he replies to their cry for an end to the hardships with threats of even larger penalties (see 1 Kings 12:12-20).

THE END OF SOLOMON'S REIGN

Was Rehoboam's response just human error? The biblical historian answer is no. Rehoboam's error in judgment is seen as the working out of the will of God (see 1 Kings 12:15). The plan of God was to punish Solomon for his worship of the gods of his foreign wives (see 1 Kings 11:33).

Our biblical writer has no doubts about God's jealous call for the exclusive loyalty of the Hebrew people. Nothing could be allowed to interfere with the primacy of their commitment to God. God alone is to be worshiped and obeyed. When the people, in the person of their royal ruler (Solomon), do not give their exclusive loyalty to God, disaster follows.

The calamity comes with a terrible, painful effect. The kingdom is divided (1 Kings 12:16-20). The temple and the palace are sacked by enemies from Egypt (1 Kings 14:25-27), and the gold and the possible golden era are gone!

■ **1 Kings 14–16.** Following the division of the kingdom in 922 BC, each of the two resulting smaller nations was ruled by a succession of kings.

The kings of Judah, the Southern Kingdom, are all descendants of Solomon and David. Rehoboam, the son of Solomon, is king when the division takes place. He rules from 922 to 915 BC. He is followed, in turn, by:

Abijah, 915–913 BC
Asa, 913–873 BC
Jehoshaphat, 873–849 BC
Jehoram, 849–843 BC

In the same period Israel, the Northern Kingdom, is ruled by Jeroboam (922–901 BC). He is not a son of Solomon but is an exile from Solomon's wrath. (Solomon heard the prophecy that Jeroboam would be king of Israel.) He comes from exile in Egypt to lead the revolt against the house of David. Jeroboam is followed, in turn, by:

Nadab, 901–900 BC
Baasha, 900–877 BC
Elah, 877–876 BC
Zimri, 876 BC
Omri, 876–869 BC
Ahab, 869–850 BC

Notice that these rulers are not all from the same family, and a number of them are assassinated. During the reign of Ahab, the last ruler of Israel in these chapters, Elijah comes to prominence as a spokesperson for God.

This ancient history and the ancient quarrels that, in Israel at least, produced such a rapid turnover of royal rulers may seem far removed from us. Do these events have a meaning for us?

Yes; if we read the passages carefully, we can discover the close relationship between the character of the kings and the quality of the peoples' lives. For the biblical historian this connection is clear and direct. When the ruler is faithful to God, all is well with the people. When the ruler's loyalties are mixed and he or she ignores God or worships other gods, then some calamity will happen to the nation. In Dimension Three, we will examine the further meaning of this reading of political history and its importance for us today.

When evaluating the reigns of these twelve rulers, two tests can be applied: (1) Does the ruler reject pagan worship practices? and (2) Is the worship of God centralized at Jerusalem, where its purity may be controlled?

How do the kings of Judah rate? Rehoboam and Abijah are failures (see 1 Kings 14:23-24; 15:3). Asa, grandson of Rehoboam, restores purity of worship but is not without fault (1 Kings 15:14). We will cover the reign of Jehoshaphat in 1 Kings 22:43-44, and of Jehoram in 2 Chronicles 21:20.

So much for the rulers of Judah. What about Israel? The story of the Northern Kingdom is one of intrigue, murder, rebellion, and constantly recurring spiritual infidelity.

THE END OF SOLOMON'S REIGN

Jeroboam's sin is judged so great that it merits extermination of his family (1 Kings 13:33-34). Nadab, his son, is also a failure (1 Kings 15:25-26). His throne is taken from him by Baasha, and the family of Jeroboam is destroyed (1 Kings 15:27-30). The twenty-four-year reign of Baasha is marked by sin, too. His son, Elah, holds the throne for two years and, while drunk, is assassinated by Zimri, an army officer. Zimri, in turn, holds onto the throne for seven days (see 1 Kings 16:15)! His brief reign ends with suicide.

The Bible tells us that Omri, who took the throne from Zimri, "sinned more than all those before him" (1 Kings 16:25). That record is repeated by his son, Ahab (see 1 Kings 16:29-34).

■ **1 Kings 17–20.** A sense of relief comes to us as we turn to look at the work of Elijah. The life of this man was lived out in the midst of an intensely gloomy period in the history of the Hebrew people.

First Kings 16:29-34 concisely recounts the evil of Ahab's reign. It comes to a climax with the practice of child sacrifice at the foundation of a city, Jericho.

Verse 34 tells us that during Ahab's reign Jericho was built "at the cost of" two children: the children of Hiel of Bethel. This notation is a reference to Joshua 6:26, in which Joshua lays a curse upon the person who rebuilds Jericho. Child sacrifice was a facet of the pagan religions that surrounded the Hebrew people. The story of Hebrew rejection of this practice is found in Genesis 22:1-14. In the story of Abraham, we learn that God does not require the blood-sacrifice of our children. In the New Testament, we discover that God intends to give Jesus' life as a sacrifice for the life of the people.

Ahab's worship of Baal is to be punished. The announcement of that judgment is made by the prophet Elijah. The time is shortly after 868 BC. Three great symbolic moments in Elijah's ministry are recounted for us in chapter 17. Verse 1 begins the record of the great drought. The story of the miracle of the meal and the oil is told in verses 7-14.

And finally, the widow's son is raised to life in verses 17-24. Notice that two of these miracles are miracles of renewal. We might even say that they are miracles of resurrection. Only one of them is an act of judgment.

Two great religious-political events of Elijah's ministry are also in these chapters: the confrontation of Elijah and Ahab, culminating in the defeat of the Baal prophets on Mount Carmel (ch. 18); and the meeting of God with Elijah at Mount Horeb (ch. 19).

The miracles and the political events tell us much of the moral, spiritual, and religious content of Elijah's message. Elijah affirms the power of God and God's involvement in the affairs of the chosen people (see 1 Kings 17:1, 17-24). Elijah also shows that commitment to God gives persons courage to face some difficult and trying times. He faces King Ahab and refuses to be called a "troubler of Israel" (18:17). He insists that the royal family, flagrant in its disobedience to God, is the source of Israel's trouble (see 1 Kings 18:17-18).

Elijah's message is dramatized through events that remind us of the signs performed by Jesus and recorded in the Gospel of John (see John 2:1-11; 4:46-54; 11:1-45). The signs of Elijah speak of God's power, judgment, concern for human need, and God's ultimate victory in the struggle for human loyalty and obedience.

Elijah remains human despite his strength, force, and faith. Fear and resignation overwhelm him when he thinks he is going to be killed (1 Kings 19:3-4). At the end of his life, Elijah accepts graciously the thought that his own work will cease and another will carry on (see 1 Kings 19:15-21).

DIMENSION THREE: WHAT DOES THE BIBLE MEAN TO ME?

We can *understand* the Bible, and we can *stand under* the Bible's message. We can learn of the character of God,

THE END OF SOLOMON'S REIGN

God's involvement in human affairs, and God's will for us. Today's chapters, 1 Kings 10–20, can be for us the word of God.

1 Kings 12:1-20—The Effects of Leadership

Ancient rulers such as Rehoboam affected the lives of their people by the way they ruled. In the same way, those who rule over us affect, for good or ill, the total life of our people.

Modern persons probably do not think that rulers alone are responsible for the evil that befalls nations. Do evil people produce evil rulers? Are the leaders in our government who practice deceit, malice, and unrestrained pride and ambition only reflecting the flaws of the people who elect them?

1 Kings 14-16—The Constancy of God

The meaning of these chapters is not in the historical details. The great lesson is the urgency confronting a favored people to remain true to the highest insights of their national history. A later message from Isaiah (see Isaiah 51:1) is as pertinent for us today as it might have been for ancient Hebrews. God was and is the "rock" and "quarry" that the prophet mentions. God gave the Israelites their life as a people, freed them from slavery, and established them in their own land. In what ways is God also our rock and quarry today?

1 Kings 17-20—The Faith of Elijah

We cannot expect Old Testament personalities to reflect the mind of Christ. We are the people who are called to adhere to the mind of Christ: "have the same mindset as Christ Jesus" (Philippians 2:5).

Although they are separated by centuries, the Christian faith and Elijah's faith are similar in important ways. We live by faith that God is active in the affairs of humanity. We know this active presence of God as the Holy Spirit. God calls us to seek close parallels between our lives and the life of Jesus (see John 14:26; 15:26; 16:14).

How can we stand against the evil in our land as Elijah stood against Ahab and Jezebel? How can we make our lives signs of the kingdom of God in the midst of humankind? How can we "signify" the way life must be lived if the world is to survive and thrive?

The spirit of Elijah is resting on Elisha. (2:15)

ELIJAH AND ELISHA
1 Kings 21–2 Kings 8

DIMENSION ONE: WHAT DOES THE BIBLE SAY?

Answer these questions by reading 1 Kings 21

1. What does Ahab do when he is denied Naboth's vineyard? (21:4)

2. For what sin does Elijah rebuke King Ahab? (21:17-20)

3. How is Ahab to be punished? (21:20-24)

4. Why does God delay this punishment? (21:27-29)

Answer these questions by reading 1 Kings 22

5. Why does Ahab hate the prophet Micaiah? (22:8)

6. What happens when Ahab disregards Micaiah's message? (22:34-40)

7. What is the character of Jehoshaphat's reign? (22:41-46)

8. What is the character of Ahaziah's reign over Israel? (22:51-53)

Answer these questions by reading 2 Kings 1–5

9. Why does Ahaziah die? (1:1-17)

10. What are some of the miracles Elisha performs? (4:1-44)

11. What kind of faith does the Shunammite woman have? (4:22-30)

12. What miracles does Elisha do with food? (4:38-44)

13. What disease does Naarnan have? (5:1)

14. Why do Elisha's instructions for his healing offend Naaman? (5:1-13)

15. Why does Naaman want to take Israelite soil home? (5:15-17)

16. How is Elisha's servant punished for his greed? (5:26-27)

Answer these questions by reading 2 Kings 7–8

17. When the people with leprosy discover the abandoned Aramean camp, what wrong do they feel they have done? (7:9)

18. What does Elisha say Hazael will do to Israel? (8:12)

19. How does Hazael get the throne of Aram for himself? (8:15)

20. Why does God continue to show mercy to the kingdom of Judah? (8:19)

21. When Jehoram fights the Edomites, what does his army do? (8:20-21)

22. What does it mean to walk in the ways of the kings of Israel? (8:18, 27)

DIMENSION TWO: WHAT DOES THE BIBLE MEAN?

■ **The Challenge of Reading Biblical History.** A constant challenge is before us as we read and study the historical books of the Bible. There is a very important response to these books that we need to make as individual readers and in our Bible study classes. This is more than some kind of memorization ordeal.

We are not required to master the ancient, sometimes confusing, and often puzzling record that we find. We do not need to find some way to accept each detail of this record as literal, historical truth. All history is written from a perspective!

The modern Christian reader has little difficulty accepting the record of events that First and Second Kings contains. Where the thoughtful Christian reader may experience difficulty is in acceptance of some of the biblical interpretations of events. To understand that statement, one has only to ask, "To what extent can a Christian mind, steeped in the thought of Jesus as displayed for us in the New Testament Gospels, accept various Old Testament pictures of God as angry, vindictive, and causing skin disease and tragic death?"

Our challenge is threefold:

1. We must search these records for the "vision of God" that is recorded for us. We must learn how the men and women of the Old Testament understood God.

2. We must search these records (the Old Testament history) to discover the similarity of this ancient vision of God to, and its contrast with, the Christian understanding of God. Anyone who has pondered seriously the meaning of Hebrews 1:1-2 can expect a fuller understanding of God than is disclosed in the Old Testament. At times we may, with deepest reverence, feel that the Old Testament understanding of God does not measure up to "the light of the knowledge of God's glory displayed in the face of Christ" (see 2 Corinthians 4:6).

A warning is needed, however. When we are reverently making such distinctions as these, we have to be careful that we do not substitute a sentimental concept of God for the awesome portrait of God as powerful, jealous, compelling, and unwaveringly moral that is so much a part of the biblical witness.

That idea is illustrated in C. S. Lewis's autobiography, *Surprised by Joy*: "The hardness of God is kinder than the softness of men, and His compulsion is our liberation."[1]

Perhaps we take offense at some of the seemingly harsh elements we find in these books because we are not convinced that it is a matter of life or death whether men and women really do belong to God. Does a portrait of God who judges persons and finds them wanting offend us because, in the end, we suspect that it doesn't really matter? Do we really think that God "by any other name" will do, like Shakespeare's rose?

3. The third aspect of our challenge in reading of these ancient historical works is to inquire earnestly what is required of us as Christian disciples in modern America.

In this spirit we may ask, "What does the Bible mean?"

■ **1 Kings 21.** This famous passage may be read in tandem with 2 Samuel 12:1-12. In each passage, a powerful ruler takes cruel, unfair advantage of a subject. David desires Uriah's wife; Ahab desires Naboth's vineyard. Neither ruler, even by his own standards, has a right to what he desires.

In each passage, we are treated to the story of a man with many resources who is not content with what he has. When having something is what life is all about, we can never have enough. In each passage, someone at hand will cater to these unlawful desires and help the ruler obtain what he wants. Also in each passage, either Nathan or Elijah is present to speak for God, advocating a better way.

These two incidents represent a great moment in Israel's religious life when a spokesperson for God challenges and rebukes a powerful political figure. This religion does not support the status quo.

In our Christian discipleship, there is an important place for praising God with our voices. But that praise of the Almighty must always be supported by the praise of lives that are faithful and obedient to God's will.

---

1 C. S. Lewis, *Surprised by Joy* (New York: HarperCollins, 1955), 280.

DIMENSION THREE: WHAT DOES THE BIBLE MEAN TO ME?

1 Kings 21:17-29—God's Moral Laws

Out of many events in these ten chapters that could be emphasized, we have chosen to focus upon Elijah's challenge to Ahab. This is a moment in Hebrew religious development when the all-powerful political entity stood on one side of a great divide while the spokesperson for God stood on the other side.

This passage is important because it insists that no person, regardless of the exalted position he or she may occupy, is above the moral laws of God. Part of the grandeur and glory of a democratic nation like ours is that, at least in theory, the same principle applies to our lives.

One of the continuously vexing problems that confronts Christians is pointed to in Jesus' words, "Give back to Caesar what is Caesar's, and to God what is God's" (Matthew 22:21; see also Romans 13:7). If the problem is only a matter of taxes for the state and tithes for the church, we can settle it simply. But a complex world like ours will not let us off quite that easily!

Dimension Two suggests parallels between 1 Kings 21 and a similar event that occurs during the reign of David. If we turn those parallels into a series of questions, with each question designed to draw us into self-examination, perhaps we can arrive at some understanding of what the Bible may mean for us.

What is the proper use of power? Every person, at one point or another in his or her life, exercises some degree of power over other persons. If nothing else, there is a time in the lives of our children when we are the authority to which they must respond. Many of us move into other areas—some quite wide, others quite limited—where we have power over other persons and circumstances.

David and Ahab were two such persons who had great amounts of power. In the incidents under review, they used their power to satisfy personal whims. They did not seem to care what happened in the lives of the persons against whom the power was used.

What motives do we have in the exercise of power? What motive does our church have as, from time to time, it exerts political, economic, or moral power? Do we have the will to touch human life in general, and human lives in particular, in ways that bring people nearer to fuller personhood?

How can we distinguish between lawful and unlawful desires? Can a person be so preoccupied with possessions that the real person dies? Is this what is meant by Jesus' parable of the rich fool (Luke 12:13-23)? Do we as Christians really believe that life is more than food, clothing, real estate, travel, sex, status, power, leisure, recreation, and titles? Or are we just kidding ourselves? How can we discipline ourselves so we do not fall victim to unlawful desires?

The king of Assyria captured Samaria and deported the Israelites to Assyria. (17:6)

4

THE DECLINE OF ISRAEL

2 Kings 9–17

DIMENSION ONE: WHAT DOES THE BIBLE SAY?

Answer these questions by reading 2 Kings 9

1. When Joram dies, what prediction comes true? (9:22-26)

2. What happens to Jezebel? (9:30-37)

Answer these questions by reading 2 Kings 10

3. How many sons of Ahab does Jehu have killed? (10:7)

4. Why does Jehu destroy the family of Ahab? (10:17)

5. How does Jehu trick the Baal worshipers? (10:18-20)

6. How does Jehu rid Israel of Baal worship? (10:24-27)

THE DECLINE OF ISRAEL

7. How does Jehu sin? (10:29)

8. Does Jehu follow all the laws of God? (10:31)

Answer these questions by reading 2 Kings 11

9. Who is queen over Judah for six years? (11:3)

10. Who leads the revolt against that queen? (11:4-13)

11. What does Jehoiada do after Athaliah has been killed? (11:17)

12. What happens to Baal worship when Joash becomes king? (11:18)

Answer these questions by reading 2 Kings 12

13. What problems does Joash have with the priests? (12:6-8)

14. How does Joash respond to Hazael's threat? (12:17-18)

15. How does Joash die? (12:20-21)

Answer these questions by reading 2 Kings 13

16. Why is Israel defeated in the time of King Jehoahaz? (13:2-3)

17. When Elisha is dying, what does he predict? (13:14-19)

18. What happens to the man being buried? (13:20-21)

Answer these questions by reading 2 Kings 14–15

19. What law of Moses does Amaziah observe? (14:5-6)

20. What illness does Azariah have? (15:5)

Answer these questions by reading 2 Kings 17

21. Why are the people punished? (17:7-9)

22. When do Israel's troubles begin? (17:21-23)

DIMENSION TWO: WHAT DOES THE BIBLE MEAN?

■ **2 Kings 9:1–10:36.** Jehu is appointed king at the command of the prophet Elisha. Jehu then immediately proceeds to assassinate Joram, the king of Israel, and Ahaziah, king of Judah. Jezebel is also killed, her body devoured by dogs; and thus the terrible curse of Elijah is fulfilled (2 Kings 9:30-37).

Jehu's vendetta against the Ahab family continues. Jehu arranges for the execution of every male of the royal family that he has superseded. Seventy sons of Ahab are killed (2 Kings 10:7), and forty-two of Ahaziah's kinsmen are put to death.

THE DECLINE OF ISRAEL

The massacres continue. Eighty soldiers are assigned to kill all the priests, worshipers, and prophets of Baal. Thus Jehu "destroyed Baal worship in Israel" (2 Kings 10:28).

God is described as pleased with Jehu's activities, but Jehu himself is not regarded as a flawless follower of the Lord and continues to sin (2 Kings 10:29-31). His career is summed up in the typical Deuteronomic manner by a formal obituary notice and the name of his successor (see 2 Kings 10:34-46).

■ **2 Kings 11:1–17:40.** These chapters take us to the year 722 BC, when the kingdom of Israel ends (2 Kings 17:1-5). The people then go into Assyrian exile.

For the biblical writers, the reason for the Exile is clear. The reason is stated in 2 Kings 17:7-8: The people have sinned under the leadership of their kings. The catalogue of sins includes the use of phallic symbols, incense burned before idols, worship of golden calves, child sacrifice, and divination and witchcraft (see 2 Kings 17:10-17). All these sins are taking place in a nation that is in covenant with God!

■ **2 Kings 14:1-6.** These verses represent a great step forward in the Hebrew understanding of God's requirements. When Amaziah comes to the throne of Judah, he proceeds to have his father's murderers put to death (2 Kings 14:5). But he stops there. He does not put to death the children of the murderers. That would be the old way. He remembers and practices the law that makes every person responsible for his or her own sins. Innocent children are not to be killed for the sins of their parents.

Amaziah's attitude reminds us of what Jeremiah later is to write concerning a new and inner covenant between God and the chosen people (see Jeremiah 31:31-34). Amaziah's action here is a moral step forward because he is rejecting the old folk proverb that says, "The parents have eaten sour grapes, / and the children's teeth are set on edge" (Jeremiah 31:29; Ezekiel 18:1-4). This introduction of the moral responsibility to God (and before God) of each individual constitutes a high point in the Hebrew understanding

35

of faithful servanthood to God. Amaziah probably did not work out this idea in depth, but he does have here the beginning of a new level of emphasis on individual responsibility in the context of community.

DIMENSION THREE: WHAT DOES THE BIBLE MEAN TO ME?

Each devout reader of the Bible finds, at each reading, some new meaning that speaks to his or her life. These nine chapters of political strife; bloodshed; the rise and fall of kings, most of them not really different from the king before; and the harlot-like disobedience of the nation can suggest much for us in modern America.

2 Kings 9:1–10:36—Understanding God's Purposes

Accounts such as the many massacres of Jehu present a dilemma for the thoughtful Christian reader. Can God really be pleased with the kind of holocaust that Jehu created?

What seems to be a conflict between the Hebrew understanding of God and our present-day Christian awareness of God is really a matter of understanding the means God approves. God's purpose is to have a people committed to the Lord and to the Lord's service alone (Exodus 20:2-17; 1 Kings 8:60-61), a "royal priesthood, a holy nation" (1 Peter 2:9).

We know that in light of Christ, God's method of winning people is the way of suffering love and service (see John 3:16). Jehu, and most of the devout worshipers of his day, saw through a mirror dimly. But in the light of Christ we see something higher, different, and better (see 1 Corinthians 13:12).

We are privileged to know that God's method is not one of bloodshed and plunder, no matter how we might be tempted to think so! God's method to win the chosen

THE DECLINE OF ISRAEL

people today imitates the manner and spirit of Jesus Christ (see John 20:21). We are to be in the world and to go in the world in the manner and spirit of Jesus of Nazareth (see Philippians 2:5-8).

How can we distinguish between our understanding of God's ultimate purpose and any particular course of action we might choose to achieve that purpose? When have you confused your action with God's purpose? We are right to believe that we can be collaborators with God. But do we always have a clear message from God concerning particular attitudes and actions? Sometimes our attitudes are based on what people say and not on what the Lord says.

We must be alert to the imperfections of pride, prejudice, greed, and hate that can shape our plans of action. We must remember that perfection in wisdom, love, goodness, grace, and truth belongs to God alone.

What of the varied religious movements of our time? What of Jehu do we see in these movements? What do we see of the mind of Christ? How can we apply that dual test to the staid, mainline churches? To the coming and going of various spiritual life groups? To the resurgence of the charismatic movement? To social-action enthusiasts? To the so-called religious right? Do any of these religious movements wholly reflect the mind and character of God?

2 Kings 11:1–17:4—Living in Exile

We Christians have New Testament authority for profound emphasis upon the mercy and forgiveness of God. God is rich in mercy (see Ephesians 2:4)! But these chapters challenge us to ask whether all sin ultimately exacts a penalty. We know the familiar words, "The one who sins is the one who will die" (Ezekiel 18:4). What of the nation that sins? What of the church that loses its first love (see Psalm 127:1; Revelation 2:4-5)?

We can go further and ask, in the depths of our hearts: Am I in exile from my own rightful place because of unfaithfulness to God as known through Jesus Christ? What is "the place" where I ought to be as a Christian? What is the significance of such biblical passages as 2 Kings 17:23; John 1:14; 14:9; 2 Corinthians 4:6? Am I missing the power for effective living that is in the godliness I profess? Am I in exile from God? From the peace and joy of believing? From fully sharing in God's distribution of the varied gifts of the Spirit (see 1 Corinthians 12:4-11)? Am I in exile from possession of the higher gifts (see 1 Corinthians 12:31-13:3)? Is life my aim? Do I long for a relationship to the church, the body of Christ?

2 Kings 14:1-6—Responsibility for Sin

Amaziah returns to the insight of Deuteronomy 24:16. The terrible happenings of Joshua 7:24-27, when Achan's family is killed, and 2 Kings 9:26, when Naboth's family is killed, are not to be repeated. In the end, of course, Amaziah himself was killed. But at this point, he steps forward to an awareness of a great basic principle of personal, rather than exclusively group-based, responsibility for sin. At the end of each day, we are questioned concerning what we did with life's challenges and opportunities. It is an awesome thing for us to know, as the spiritual has it, "It's me, O Lord, standing in the need of prayer!" We are filled with fear and trembling to know that we are dealing with a God who sees us (see 1 Samuel 16:7; Isaiah 29:15; Romans 8:27; Psalm 139:1- 13)! How can we make Psalm 139:23-24 the earnest prayer for this hour?

So Judah went into captivity, away from her land. (25:21)

5
THE KINGDOM OF JUDAH
2 Kings 18–25

DIMENSION ONE:
WHAT DOES THE BIBLE SAY?

Answer these questions by reading 2 Kings 18

1. Why does Hezekiah break the bronze snake Moses made? (18:4)

2. What reward does Hezekiah's devotion to God bring? (18:7)

3. What happens to the Israelites when Samaria (Israel) is conquered? (18:11)

4. Why does this happen to Israel? (18:12)

5. How does Hezekiah respond to Sennacherib's attack? (18:13-16)

GENESIS to REVELATION **2 KINGS**

Answer these questions by reading 2 Kings 19–20

6. How does Isaiah encourage Hezekiah? (19:6-7)

7. How does Isaiah act as Hezekiah's physician? (20:7)

8. What sign is given that God will heal Hezekiah? (20:8-11)

9. How does Hezekiah accept Babylon's final victory? (20:16-19)

Answer these questions by reading 2 Kings 21–22

10. What evils does Manasseh commit? (21:1-7, 16)

11. Who follows Manasseh as king? (22:1)

12. Who is Hilkiah? (22:8)

13. What does Hilkiah find? (22:8-10)

14. How does Josiah respond to this important find? (22:11)

Answer these questions by reading 2 Kings 23

15. What sexual act of worship does Josiah banish? (23:7)

THE KINGDOM OF JUDAH

16. Where are child sacrifices usually made? (23:10)

17. What religious festival does Josiah renew? (23:21-22)

18. How does the biblical writer summarize Josiah's reign? (23:25)

19. How does the Lord feel about Judah? (23:26-27)

20. With whom is God most angry? (23:26-27)

21. Where are the rest of the acts of Josiah written? (23:28)

22. Who kills King Josiah? (23:29-30)

Answer these questions by reading 2 Kings 24–25

23. What foreign king exacts Judah's submission? (24:1)

24. Who remains in the land after Nebuchadnezzar captures Jerusalem? (24:10-16)

25. What happens to Jehoiachin after thirty-seven years of exile? (25:27-30)

DIMENSION TWO: WHAT DOES THE BIBLE MEAN?

We are coming rapidly to the end of the Southern Kingdom (Judah). Today's chapters carry us from the reign of Hezekiah in Judah to the destruction of the temple. We see the fall of Jerusalem and the last sad days of the last king of Judah.

The time spans from about 725 BC to about 586 BC. In this one hundred thirty-nine-year span, eight kings ascend and leave the throne of Judah. True to the spirit of Deuteronomy, our biblical writers do not hesitate to assess the influence and the character of these kings. Only two of them—Hezekiah and Josiah—are described as rulers who did what was pleasing in the sight of the Lord. The others—Manasseh, Amon, Jehoahaz, Jehoiakim, Jehoiachin, Zedekiah—are judged harshly in that they "did evil in the eyes of the LORD" (2 Kings 24:19).

Perhaps we need to offer a word about the assignment of dates to biblical events. The research tools of biblical historical scholars do not permit precise pinpointing of dates in many instances. But the variation in dates is not significant enough to hinder our attempt to grasp the Bible's meaning.

Only two good kings reign in a period of one hundred thirty-nine years. Six evil kings reign during the same time span. We shall see that the good ones, Hezekiah and Josiah, were really very good kings. Some of the wicked ones, notably Manasseh and Amon, were very evil indeed.

In these chapters, we also have our first contact with the prophet Isaiah of Jerusalem. Our best study source for this giant in Hebrew religion is chapters 1–39 of the Book of Isaiah. When we study 2 Chronicles 32, we will encounter him again.

Now let's look in detail at the work of Hezekiah and Josiah. Both of these kings "did what was right in the eyes of the LORD" (2 Kings 18:3; 22:2).

THE KINGDOM OF JUDAH

■ **2 Kings 18–20.** Some scholars date Hezekiah's reign as 716–687 BC. This reign of twenty-nine years is marked by several important factors.

Hezekiah is a righteous king. He is one of the two kings given unqualified approval by the writers of First and Second Kings (see 2 Kings 18:3, 5).

The good that Hezekiah does includes the reform of Judah's worship of God. This worship needs reform because many pagan elements, particularly idolatrous images, have been allowed to creep in during the reign of various evil rulers. He also tries to destroy the local shrines. For Hezekiah to destroy the bronze serpent, traditionally believed to have been made by Moses, shows us that he takes the reform seriously (see 2 Kings 18:4).

Hezekiah seems to enjoy considerable military success, at least for a while (see 2 Kings 18:7-8). Though he is successful in his rebellion against the king of Assyria, he is eventually reduced to the position of a vassal to Sennacherib, king of Assyria (see 2 Kings 18:13-17). Hezekiah resorts to stripping both the temple and the royal treasury of gold to pay off Sennacherib.

In his time of greatest distress, Hezekiah at last resorts to the advice of the Lord and asks for the aid of Isaiah, the prophet, a man of God. Isaiah tells Hezekiah that the Assyrian king will return to Assyria soon (see 2 Kings 19:6-7).

The Assyrians are defeated by "the angel of the Lord" when one hundred eighty-five thousand men die in a single night. So Isaiah's prophecy is fulfilled (see 2 Kings 19:35).

Isaiah heals a grave illness of Hezekiah. The "poultice of figs" was commonly used to heal boils (see 2 Kings 20:7).

In the end, Hezekiah learns from Isaiah that Judah will come to an end as Israel has already ended. He is relieved that this event will not occur during his lifetime.

What do these events all mean? Among many possible answers are these:

1. God does bless good persons in their own time. The idea that evil carries over from generation to generation

may seem to prevail. But ultimately our Christian faith teaches us that God is keeping watch.

2. Prayer and the counsel of godly persons are two rich and important resources for all of us. Whether we are kings or among the poor, we do not struggle with life's challenges alone.

3. Those persons who yearn to worship God in spirit and in truth, as Jesus urged us to do, must stay alert lest their own prayer and worship become tainted with pagan thoughts, goals, and practices.

■ **2 Kings 21.** This chapter covers the reign of Manasseh, who restored Baal worship and put an Asherah poles in the temple. He, singlehandedly, undid nearly all the good of his predecessor, Hezekiah. He did so much evil in the sight of God, that even Josiah's wonderful reforms could not save Judah from rejection (see 2 Kings 23:26-27). He was followed by his son, Amon, who was no better.

■ **2 Kings 22:1–25:30.** Josiah reigned over Judah for thirty-one years (640–609 BC). His reign, and the persons covered by his kingly authority, is blessed by the discovery of the Book of the Law in the temple. Great religious reform follows that discovery. Its implications are far-reaching for that era; there are lessons for us to learn, also.

What precisely was this Book of the Law? Biblical scholars have thought much about the particular material found by Hilkiah, the high priest (see 2 Kings 22:8). Many believe that this was what we know today as Deuteronomy 12–26 and 28. Careful reading and comparison of these chapters from our present-day Deuteronomy and the chapters of Second Kings describing King Josiah's reform show the two are very similar.

Briefly, here is what is covered in the Deuteronomy chapters:

1. The Hebrew people are to worship only one God, "the Lord, the God of your ancestors." No traces of pagan worship are to be left in the holy land (see Deuteronomy 12:1-2).

THE KINGDOM OF JUDAH

2. God is concerned that worship be conducted in a worthy spirit. The Lord is concerned with what we would term "ritual cleanliness." But God is also concerned with the rightness of relations among people (see Deuteronomy 14–15).

3. The Hebrews are always to remember God's great redemptive act, the Passover. Passover celebrates their deliverance from Egyptian slavery and is to be a central feast of their faith (see Deuteronomy 16:1-8). The festivals of their faith are a sign of their special relationship with God (Deuteronomy 16:1). In addition to Passover, these include the Feast of Weeks and the Feast of Booths.

4. Some rights of women are protected. This is a great step forward in that ancient, totally male-dominated society (see Deuteronomy 21:10-17).

5. Sexual restraint and purity are expected of the people of God (see Deuteronomy 21:10-17).

6. The cause of the poor is a concern of God (see Deuteronomy 24:10-22).

Some emphases in these chapters of Deuteronomy sound strange and even unchristian to us. We could not expect to find it otherwise. These are the laws of an ancient culture. Nevertheless, we rejoice that finding these chapters serves as the basis for a great moment of religious revival and renewal, which begins in the temple and the government. The high priest finds the written word and shares it with the king. The king has the word read in the presence of the people.

Revival and renewal come when monarch, priest, and the people alike react to the message of Deuteronomy. What they hear is God's message that all should repent (turn away from old wrongs), restore (begin again to worship God), revive (their sense of national calling to be a people holy to the Lord), and renew the covenant with God.

But these chapters of Second Kings do not promise that even this great religious revival will cancel the inevitable penalty for centuries of wrongdoing. In the end,

Jerusalem, the temple, the king's houses, and all the houses of Jerusalem were burned (see 2 Kings 25:9). The kingdom that began with Saul, and achieved glory and grandeur under David and Solomon, ends.

DIMENSION THREE: WHAT DOES THE BIBLE MEAN TO ME?

These are exciting chapters. As we read, we feel we are dealing with living history. The discovery of the law, the renewal of the nation's commitment to God, the introduction to the prophet Isaiah, and even the sad pictures of final defeat all give us a sense of something alive and moving, something that has meaning for our own existence. This sense of the Bible's aliveness leads some devout Bible readers to declare that the written words are the vehicle for the living word of God. That living word is the truth of God and the relevance of the truth of God to our own lives.

2 Kings 18:1–20:21—Being a Good Person

God is always in the business of finding, calling, and sending one good person who can help the rest of us come nearer to the divine dream for our lives. In 2 Kings 18:1–20:21, that good person is Hezekiah. The prophet Isaiah is another.

Centuries later, another man is "sent from God whose name was John" (John 1:6). In the fullness of time, there is to be a man named Jesus of Nazareth!

Poet and lyricist Vachel Lindsay (1879–1931) has described such men and women as constituting "An Endless Line of Splendor." Ask yourself: Am I a part of that line? Am I a good person? How do my presence and work help others come nearer to the divine dream for their lives?

THE KINGDOM OF JUDAH

As we honestly, earnestly seek our place in this procession of truly good persons, we may expect to receive evidence of God's presence and approval. Such evidence will not be an occasion for spiritual pride. We will resist pride as we resist the devil (see 1 Peter 5:6-9)!

For Hezekiah, these tokens included physical healing and the backward movement of the sun's shadow upon the dial (2 Kings 20:1-11). What will these tokens be for us? Perhaps for some they will be the spectacular gifts of the Spirit (see 1 Corinthians 12:10). For most of us they will more likely be the quiet, useful gifts that build up the church (see 1 Corinthians 14:12). Surely for every Christian there will be a measure of the greatest and highest gift of all, the gift of love (see 1 Corinthians 12:3–13:14).

2 Kings 22:1–25:30—Religious Revival

A tent evangelist once declared that every facet of a person's faith could be evaluated by the depth of his or her longing for a revival of religion. Would we not go a step further and declare that longing for renewal—of faith and virtue in church; of integrity in politics, in economics, and in social relationships of every type—measures the quality of an individual's religion and patriotism?

These chapters, which describe for us the great reform under Josiah, suggest important elements for renewal that might come to our own church and to our own land.

Would one element for renewal be a rediscovery of the written word of God, the Bible? How can such a rediscovery permit us to understand God's message? How can we "stand under" that message and accept its judgment and its offer of grace? What changes in our personal and community behavior will we need to make?

How should the major agencies in our society share in this renewal? For Josiah and the people of his day, those agencies were the monarchy and the priesthood. What are these agencies now? What changes can the church, government, our homes and families, the educational system, and our economic system make? All these systems need to work in harmony with one another in search of truth, creativity, compassion, and all the varied forms of healing for which church and nation alike cry out. What in our society needs to be renewed?

These were the sons of Israel. (2:1)

6

GENEALOGIES
1 Chronicles 1–8

DIMENSION ONE: WHAT DOES THE BIBLE SAY?

Answer these questions by reading 1 Chronicles 1

1. Who was the first man? (1:1)

2. Who is the Northern Kingdom named for? (1:34; 2:1)

Answer these questions by reading 1 Chronicles 2

3. How were Judah (the man) and Israel (the man) related? (2:1)

4. What two men are remembered for being evil? (2:3, 7)

5. Who are David's father, grandfather, and great-grandfather? (2:10-15)

Answer these questions by reading 1 Chronicles 3

6. How long does David rule over the United Kingdom? (3:4)

GENESIS to REVELATION 1 CHRONICLES

7. From what cities does he rule? (3:4)

8. How many generations are there from Solomon to Josiah? (3:10-14)

Answer these questions by reading 1 Chronicles 4

9. What man is remembered for his great honor? (4:9)

10. For what two things does this man ask God? (4:10)

Answer these questions by reading 1 Chronicles 5

11. Does God take sides in battle? (5:18-26)

12. How is Manasseh described for worshiping other gods? (5:25)

Answer these questions by reading 1 Chronicles 6

13. Who is Johanan? (6:10)

14. What do the men David appoints to the temple do? (6:31)

15. Who originates or founds the temple worship ritual? (6:49)

GENEALOGIES

16. Who is in charge of burnt offerings and incense offerings? (6:49)

17. Why are these offerings made? (6:49)

18. What makes the cities mentioned valuable? (6:67-81)

Answer these questions by reading 1 Chronicles 7

19. What makes these families special? (7:1-12)

20. What woman do we remember for building cities? (7:24)

Answer these questions by reading 1 Chronicles 8

21. Where do the heads of the tribe of Benjamin reside? (8:28)

22. What important king comes from the tribe of Benjamin? (8:33)

DIMENSION TWO: WHAT DOES THE BIBLE MEAN?

First and Second Chronicles are the first of four books of the Bible by a single writer: First and Second Chronicles, Ezra, and Nehemiah. The writer, whose real name is forever lost to history, is given the title "the Chronicler," from the Hebrew title of the first two of these four books. These four books repeat and extend the earlier biblical record known as the Deuteronomic history. The Deuteronomic history begins with Joshua and ends with Second Kings. It is generally believed that the Chronicler wrote in a much later time than the actual events, after the people had returned from exile.

First and Second Chronicles convey much of the same message that we have already examined in our study of First and Second Kings. We may ask, in view of our previous study of this very ancient history, whether there is something more for us to learn here. The answer is yes. First and Second Chronicles can help us fix an outline of Hebrew history a bit deeper in our minds. That outline is of significance to us only if we ask ourselves what the meaning of that history is.

What does this Chronicles history mean? We will see that it has an overall meaning and then, as we examine the record section by section, we will see that this history has many levels of meaning. We may think of the central purpose of the Chronicles history as a major river such as the Mississippi River. We may think of the tributary meanings as smaller but important rivers that contribute to that major river.

The Chronicler's main purpose is to affirm the preeminence of David and his family in establishing the Hebrew people as a political state. David established a nation essentially God-centered in its life, though it often, by reason of human sin, departed from its original high calling.

Throughout Chronicles, we shall find an emphasis upon the unity of the Hebrew people. That unity is focused in the work of one man, David; the worth of one city, Jerusalem; and the worship of God centered in one building, the temple.

David is the founder of what we might call the church of the Jews. David plans the temple, and David sets in motion the pattern of worship in the temple. In Chronicles we see the rise, decline, and final fall of David's kingdom. Through it all perhaps, as Christian readers of history before Christ, "Whether you turn to the right or to the left, your ears will

GENEALOGIES

hear a voice behind you, saying, 'This is the way; walk in it'" (Isaiah 30:21). We will look for a possible message for us as disciples of Jesus Christ as we read what the Bible says in these chapters.

■ **1 Chronicles 1–2.** Hebrew history is part of the history of the human race. The human race began, as the book of Genesis teaches us, with the man Adam.

From these descendants of Adam, namely Shem, Ham, and Japheth, come what the ancient Hebrews saw as the three major ethnic groups of humanity. These were the Japhethites, the Hamites, and the Semites (see 1 Chronicles 1:5, 8, 17).

This Chronicles history then becomes Semitic history: from Shem to Abraham to Israel to Judah (see 1 Chronicles 1:17, 28, 34; 2:1). From Judah, our historian moves across the generations to David (one feels the Chronicler sighs with relief), who at last is given charge of the kingdom (see 1 Chronicles 10:14).

First Chronicles 1–2 contain a note of universalism. God loves and cares for all humankind. That universalism is suggested by tracing the entire human race to a single beginning point. Much later, in the New Testament, we find Christ spoken of as a second Adam (see 1 Corinthians 15:45). So we are justified in saying that, as the human race had its fleshly beginning in the man Adam, so a new race has its beginning in "the last Adam," Jesus Christ. We know that in Jesus the universal love of God came to its fullest expression (see John 3:16).

■ **1 Chronicles 6.** This chapter brings us very close to one of the major interests of the Chronicler, who is deeply interested in the conduct of the worshipers in the temple; he sees worship, as far as the chapter at hand is concerned, as having two focal points: (1) the worship of God through the music of the human voice, lifted in praise, in prayer, and in supplication to Almighty God, and (2) the solemn offering of sacrifices of the burnt flesh of animals and of incense, that atonement might be made for the sin of the people.

Why is atonement necessary? Because despite all the favor with which God looks upon David, and despite the close relationship that David has with God, David is not without grievous sin. We need look only at the story of Uriah and Bathsheba for the ugly evidence (see 2 Samuel 11:1-27). Even David did something that displeased the Lord. Much of this history, what we have read and what we shall continue to read, is replete with constant infidelity, transgression, and falling away.

In order for all this sin to be overcome, there is the need for atonement. The acts of atonement are, for the Chronicler, rooted in the tradition of Moses and Aaron and in the labors of David (see 1 Chronicles 6:31-49). Thus, for the Chronicler, these marvelous provisions for materials and movement and skills and gifts, elements of the approved public worship of God, are not something new, innovative, and fleeting. This majestic yet jubilant approach to the presence of God for acts of praise, sacrifice, prayer, and petition is rooted in the very beginnings of the relationship between God and this special chosen people (see Deuteronomy 26:5- 10; 14:2; 10:12-22; 7:6-11).

Christian readers will recall the great passage in Hebrews that insists that these sacrifices, whatever their original value, are temporary or transitory (see Hebrews 9). At the end of the day, what sinful humanity needs is not the gift we bring to be offered up. What we must have to perfect the conscience of the worshiper is the "blood of Christ . . . offered . . . unblemished to God" (Hebrews 9:14). What we must have is some mighty act of God, beyond law and our own performance, to place us in right relationship with the Lord (see Romans 3:20-26).

■ **1 Chronicles 7–8.** Here we read the genealogies of the tribes of Issachar, Zebulun, Naphtali, Manasseh, Ephraim, Asher, and Benjamin. Although 7:6 mentions the name *Benjamin*, the original text probably contained the word *Zebulun*. The names of these two tribes are similar in Hebrew.

DIMENSION THREE: WHAT DOES THE BIBLE MEAN TO ME?

1 Chronicles 1–2—Universalism

The idea of universalism as explored here is not the theological concept regarding an anticipated outcome of the universe, that all will be reconciled to God in the end whether they believed in God or not. As we are discussing it here, universalism is not looking forward, but looking back on our history at where we have come from. Our communal heritage traced back to Adam provides us with an understanding that God's love is an inclusive love that connects us to all of humanity. God is concerned with the entire human race, not just the chosen Israelites. Do you believe God cares for every person on earth? How would it change our response to one another if we truly believed each person to be a beloved child of God?

1 Chronicles 6:31-48—Worshiping God

Consider the nature of a religious experience and the character of a structured religion that has within it constant chords of joyous praise, solemn prayer, penitence, victory, longing, defeat, hope, and certainty. What is the meaning of a religious experience when we find these characteristics in the context of singing and playing instruments? (Think of all the references to musical instruments in Psalm 150; read of the priests sounding trumpets in 1 Chronicles 16:6.) What are the characteristics of the worship we offer to God in our time?

To what understanding of the character of God did the Hebrew people respond as they worshiped? To God's power? To God's acts to deliver them from slavery and establish them in a land of their own (see Exodus 3:7-18)? The early Israelites saw themselves in a favored position.

How did this view affect their response to God? To what in the character of God do we respond as we worship?

1 Chronicles 6:49—Atonement Comes From God

We noted in Dimension Two the need to understand *atonement* in Christian terms. In this passage in First Chronicles, the writer reminds us that Aaron and his sons were responsible for the atonement of all the Israelites. To bring about this atonement, the Aaronites presented burnt and incense offerings on behalf of all the people.

What does the word *atonement* mean for Christians today? We can best understand this concept if we describe it as something that makes us "at one" with God. Atonement occurs when the wall of hostility (rebellion, disobedience, or neglect of conscious attention to God) is broken down. Atonement comes to us from an action of God. It is not our gift that makes us at one with God. It is God's gift of Jesus Christ.

Aaron and his sons made atonement for the people as a whole. For what sins do we, as a people, need atonement? For what sins do you need atonement? How does God's gift of Jesus Christ atone for your sins?

*And David became more and more powerful, because the
LORD Almighty was with him. (11:9)*

7

DAVID, THE GREAT KING

1 Chronicles 9–14

DIMENSION ONE: WHAT DOES THE BIBLE SAY?

Answer these questions by reading 1 Chronicles 9

1. What are the three kinds of servants for the house of the Lord? (9:10, 14, 17)

2. Who appoints gatekeepers for the house of the Lord? (9:22-23)

3. Where do the Levitical temple guards and singers live? (9:27, 33)

Answer these questions by reading 1 Chronicles 10

4. Why does Saul kill himself? (10:4-5)

5. What do the Philistines do with Saul's body? (10:8-10)

6. How does the Chronicler interpret Saul's death? (10:13-14)

7. To whom does the Lord give the kingdom upon Saul's death? (10:14)

Answer these questions by reading 1 Chronicles 11

8. Where is David anointed king over Israel? (11:1-3)

9. What is David called? (11:2)

10. By what authority do the elders make David king? (11:3)

11. By what other names is Jerusalem known? (11:4-5)

12. Who is the chief of the Thirty? (11:20-21)

Answer these questions by reading 1 Chronicles 12

13. What military skill do the Benjamites have? (12:2)

14. Why does Amasai pledge loyalty to David? (12:18)

15. How is David's army increased? (12:19-22)

DAVID, THE GREAT KING

16. Why do the men of war come to Hebron? (12:38)

17. What do the people eat when they celebrate David's coronation? (12:39-40)

Answer these questions by reading 1 Chronicles 13

18. What is neglected in Saul's day? (13:3)

19. What do the people do while the ark is being taken to Jerusalem? (13:8)

20. What happens to Uzzah? (13:9-10)

21. What does God do for Obed-Edom? (13:13-14)

Answer these questions by reading 1 Chronicles 14

22. Who helps David build his capital? (14:1)

23. Where is Solomon born? (14:3-4)

24. What does God promise David? (14:9-10)

25. What do the Philistines leave at Baal Perazim? (14:12)

DIMENSION TWO: WHAT DOES THE BIBLE MEAN?

The Chronicler's view of history is that of a Levite and a member of the temple singers. The Chronicler places great emphasis upon the important role of the Levites. Equal emphasis is placed upon the place of music in the worship of God (see 1 Chronicles 9:2, 14, 26, 33). The Chronicler values the high privilege of the Levites as they lead the congregation of Israel in their prayer and praise addressed to God (see 1 Chronicles 16:4; 23:30).

The Chronicler reveres David as a founder of the Jewish worshiping community. The role of David in establishing Jerusalem as the Holy City is also emphasized by the Chronicler. David is credited with establishing the pattern for the temple worship (see 1 Corinthians 9:22; 11:4-9; 13:1-4; 14:1-3).

The Chronicler also has a definite view of the nature and character of God. God demands exclusive loyalty from those who have entered into a covenant relationship. Saul's death illustrates the dangers of not being totally and exclusively loyal to God (see 1 Chronicles 10:13-14). David's role in Hebrew life and history is the result of God's personal choice (see 1 Chronicles 11:1-2). God joins the chosen and faithful people in their war against those who are pagans (see 1 Chronicles 11:9, 14; 14:10-11).

Another area the Chronicler places great emphasis upon is the unity of the Hebrew people. They are one people because they are in covenant with the one true God. They worship God in the one true way and at the one true place. They are one people because there is one man (David) who, with his descendants, is appointed by God to rule over them.

Today's chapters point to each of these emphases. We shall, in the weeks ahead, become even more aware of these traits of the Chronicler's faith.

DAVID, THE GREAT KING

When we ask, "What does the Bible mean?" our question is twofold: (1) What do we think this recital of history meant to its first readers? and (2) What does this history mean to us now?

■ **1 Chronicles 9:1-44.** Worship in the temple is carefully planned and becomes possible because of the labors of many persons. All have a cherished role to play. Color, movement, music, incense, and other symbols are part of praise and thanksgiving to God. Psalm 67:3-5 is descriptive of the attitude toward worship at that time.

■ **1 Chronicles 10.** Again, a mysterious emphasis is placed upon the terrible demands God makes on the chosen people. We have to ask whether verse 14 is acceptable to the Christian mind as an accurate reflection of God's character.

■ **1 Chronicles 11–14.** David is king, presiding over the affairs of his people. We studied this history earlier in 2 Samuel 5.

■ **1 Chronicles 13.** The Christian can well ponder this chapter. The ark symbolizes the presence of God with the people. Because the law is stored within the ark, it speaks also of the covenant relationship between this people and the living God.

■ **1 Chronicles 14.** This section closes with an idyllic picture of David as prosperous, secure in the loyalty and affection of his people, and blessed in his personal life.

DIMENSION THREE: WHAT DOES THE BIBLE MEAN TO ME?

Among many of the possible meanings of today's Bible chapters, we may consider these: (1) What do these chapters say to us about the Old Testament and New Testament worship of God? and (2) What do these chapters require us to ask ourselves about our own present-day religion?

1 Chronicles 9:17-34—Worship in the Old Testament

Desirable worship may use forms of ritual, song, musical instruments, and dance. God accepts this type of worship. However, such worship must be offered in a context of daily living marked by justice, mercy, and humility.

The Chronicler's work makes us aware of the importance of public worship offered by the assembled congregation. But we must balance the Chronicler's emphasis upon the rituals of worship with the prophetic insistence upon justice, mercy, and humility as part of that worship. This is the spirit and truth that God calls for (see Amos 5:21-24; Hosea 6:4-6; Micah 6:8; John 4:23-24).

In examining the Hebrew worship as described by the Chronicler and the various psalmists, we learn that many persons are involved in or participate in worship. They are not just spectators. These are all men and women who lead the worshiping congregation. However, they do not relieve the people of their right and privilege to worship. It is the congregation that joins in the praise of God, in the celebration of God's goodness, in the remembrance of God's past mercies, and in the joyful anticipation of the goodness yet to come from God's hand.

This passage in First Chronicles invites us to evaluate our care for the place of meeting and our concern for the quality of worship offered by the congregation. How much adornment of the house of worship is needed? Is it as possible to spend too little on our church houses as it is possible to spend too much on them? If there is a beauty of holiness, is there also a holiness of beauty?

1 Chronicles 13—The Ark's Resting Place

The ark was the throne of God and the supreme symbol of the presence of God. It spoke in thunderous tones of silence concerning God's covenant with Israel and the bestowal of the law upon them. Here, the ark finds a resting place as David has it placed in a specially prepared tent.

What are the central symbols in the place where your congregation gathers to worship? Do a cross, a pulpit, and a Communion Table stand in close relationship at the front of the sanctuary? What other items are present, and what is the significance of these items?

What does the Communion Table call to mind? Is God willing to meet us in fellowship there? Why is the pulpit so prominent? Do we worship a God who communicates? How is God's will made known to us?

How should we come into the presence of God? What is the proper attitude for worship? Is the answer given by Micah sufficient (see Micah 6:6-8)? Do we need also to sing, laugh, lift our hands, shout our praise, bend our bodies in prayer, and make gifts for God? When and how is God rightly worshiped?

GENESIS to REVELATION **1 CHRONICLES**

I will set him over my house and my kingdom forever; his throne will be established forever. (17:14)

THE ARK OF THE COVENANT

1 Chronicles 15–21

DIMENSION ONE: WHAT DOES THE BIBLE SAY?

Answer these questions by reading 1 Chronicles 15

1. Who carries the ark? (15:2)

2. Where is the ark? (15:25)

3. How are the people who carry the ark dressed? (15:27)

4. What are the people doing as they bring up the ark? (15:28)

Answer these questions by reading 1 Chronicles 16

5. Where does the ark first rest? (16:1)

THE ARK OF THE COVENANT

6. When David completes the offerings, what does each worshiper receive? (16:3)

7. What do the Levites who minister before the ark do? (16:4-6)

8. What does Asaph sing about? (16:8, 12)

9. Who gives the Hebrews their homeland? (16:14-18)

10. What are the worshipers to bring as they come before the Lord? (16:29)

Answer these questions by reading 1 Chronicles 17

11. What kind of house does David live in? (17:1)

12. What does God tell Nathan to tell David? (17:3-5)

13. Who will build a house for God? (17:11-12)

14. How does David feel about God's promises? (17:16-27)

Answer this question by reading 1 Chronicles 18

15. How does David reign over Israel? (18:14)

Answer these questions by reading 1 Chronicles 19

16. How do the Ammonites respond to David's sympathy when Nahash dies? (19:1-5)

17. What do the Arameans and the Ammonites do at the battle? (19:14-15)

Answer this question by reading 1 Chronicles 20

18. In what season do kings go to war? (20:1)

Answer these questions by reading 1 Chronicles 21

19. Who originates the idea of a census of Israel? (21:1)

20. Who is in charge of the census? (21:2)

21 How many men are reported in the census? (21:5)

22. What punishment does David choose? (21:13-14)

23. Where is David to build an altar to God? (21:15, 18)

24. Why does David refuse the threshing floor as a gift? (21:24)

THE ARK OF THE COVENANT

25. What does God do when David makes his offerings on this new altar? (21:26)

DIMENSION TWO: WHAT DOES THE BIBLE MEAN?

These chapters continue the idyllic picture of King David's reign that closed our last session (see 1 Chronicles 14:1, 2, 17).

■ **1 Chronicles 15.** The ark is brought from the house of Obed-Edom to Jerusalem.

■ **1 Chronicles 15:1-28.** We must remember that for the Chronicler, David is the primary example of a man who is intensely enthusiastic for God. David, despite his errors and faults, habitually turns to God in an attitude of trust, love, and humility. Many times David is shown to be a man whose emotional and spiritual life is filled with a love for God. David is grateful to God and endeavors to praise and thank the Holy One for the bounty of gifts given to him.

A major expression of David's own devotion to God comes in all that he does to establish, enrich, and further the worship of God. That fostering of the worship of God is the basic emphasis of this chapter.

The ark is brought to the city of Jerusalem, now known as "the City of David" (see 1 Chronicles 15:29). The ark must be brought by that special class of temple personnel, the Levites. These Levites are a group of village priests whose primary function is to teach religious truth. We see them functioning as persons who explain or interpret the written word of God (also see Nehemiah 8:1-8).

The Levites claim to be descended from Moses, and their task is to expound on Israel's faith (see 2 Chronicles 15:3; 17:8-9; 30:22; 35:3). Their job is not the same as that of the priests who preside at the altar. So, in Luke 10:31-32, Jesus makes a distinction between a "priest" and a "Levite."

The Levites must sanctify themselves to carry the ark for fear some disaster might befall them. Sanctifying themselves in a ritual purification may include anointing themselves with oil, praying, and making offerings to God. The ritual may also include eating sacrificial meat and a period of abstention from sexual intercourse (see Leviticus 22:1-7; 1 Samuel 21:4-6).

■ **1 Chronicles 15:29.** This verse might be titled, "When Love Becomes Contempt." Has Michal, daughter of Saul, who had once loved David so passionately, now become this disdainful because of her pride? Does she fear that a king who shares too much in the common life might lose the aura of royalty and perhaps even lose his throne (see 1 Samuel 18:20)?

■ **1 Chronicles 16.** The services of the Levites before the ark are described in this chapter. Most of the chapter consists of a hymn of praise composed, in part, of other psalms. See these comparisons, for example: Psalm 105:1-15 and 1 Chronicles 16:8-22; Psalm 96:1-13 and 1 Chronicles 16:23-33; Psalm 106:1 and 1 Chronicles 16:34; and Psalm 106:47-48 and 1 Chronicles 16:35-36.

■ **1 Chronicles 17.** God refuses David's offer of a "palace of cedar" like his own. But, through the prophet Nathan, the Lord promises a great future for David's family. God also promises that one of David's own sons will be allowed to build a house for the Lord.

■ **1 Chronicles 17:1-15.** A recurring theme in the early history of the Hebrew people is the conflict between the old, nomadic life and the newer, settled life. In the past, the Hebrews had been a nomadic people, but now they have built cities and have begun an agrarian society. We see this conflict suggested in God's preference of Abel's offering over the offering of Cain (see Genesis 4:4-5). This conflict is also seen in the Rekabites, a sect in Israel who refused wine, scorned vineyards, and would not live in houses or till the soil (see Jeremiah 35). We also find this conflict here in God's preference of a tent for a dwelling place rather than a house.

THE ARK OF THE COVENANT

The house of the Lord will not be built in David's time. The temple will be built (as we know) by David's son Solomon, who is chosen to succeed his father.

While God rejects the offer of a house, the Lord responds freely and generously to David. God knows David's intentions are good. That response is a promise to establish David and his descendants upon Israel's throne forever.

- **1 Chronicles 17:16-27.** This section shows us a man who is overwhelmed by the generosity of God. David feels grateful, humble, and in awe of God. "Who am I ?" David asks. David is humbled by his realization of the greatness of God and the uniqueness given to his people because of their relationship to God (see 1 Chronicles 16:20-21).
- **1 Chronicles 18–20.** These chapters tell the stories of various wars David is engaged in; each time God gives him victory over the enemy. "The LORD gave David victory wherever he went" (1 Chronicles 18:13).
- **1 Chronicles 21.** In this chapter, a census is proposed by David but is resisted by Joab, his military commander. God is offended by the census and threatens destruction. After David repents, God forgives him and tells David to build an altar on the threshing floor of Araunah the Jebusite.

The opening verse of this chapter brings us face to face with questions concerning the origin of evil. Here we see "Satan" credited with the idea of the census; in 2 Samuel 24:1, David counts Israel and Judah because God is angry with Israel. The passage here reminds us of Job 1:6-12, where we find Satan among the sons of God and actually charged with, or given permission to do, a task of which God seems to approve. What is the origin of evil? This is one of the great mysteries of our life and our faith.

David repents of this grievous error and offers himself before God as the guilty one. David's act of intercession (1 Chronicles 21:17) reminds us of the words of Moses (Exodus 31:31-32), of Abraham (Genesis 18:22-23), and of Paul (Romans 9:1-3). The Christian who intercedes in prayer is in great company!

DIMENSION THREE: WHAT DOES THE BIBLE MEAN TO ME?

1 Chronicles 15:1-2—The Levites Are Sanctified

Let us ask some questions about our own feelings of what is "fit and proper" for the worship of God. What do we think is "required" of those persons who are either chosen by the community or self-chosen to handle the holy things?

Where, for example, do we assign some value to ritual cleanliness, particularly as we engage in the public worship of God? Where does the expression "Sunday clothes" come from? Why do some people tend to dress better, with special attention to cleanliness and appearance, when they attend church? Is it nothing more than a matter of keeping up with the neighbors? Or is there something deeper at the root of this practice?

We may ask more fundamental questions: What do we feel is required or desirable in the people who respond to the call of God in ministry? In the people who distribute the elements during Holy Communion? In those who pray with us at the approach of death? In persons who counsel with us on the great issues of life?

Must these persons be sanctified in character and in commitment to Christ? Is theirs a greater sanctity than the ritual holiness expected of the Levites who carried the ark? Why or why not?

What was Jesus offering to his disciples when he said, "For them I sanctify myself, that they too may be truly sanctified" (John 17:19)?

1 Chronicles 15:29—Michal's Pride

In Dimension Two, we suggested that Michal has contempt for David because her pride will not let her enjoy the experiences of the common people. If Michal is too proud for her husband, David, to share fully in the life of

THE ARK OF THE COVENANT

the common people, how does her attitude compare with that of Jesus (see Philippians 2:5-9; John 13:1-17; 21:9-13; Luke 22:24-27)? How does your pride affect your reactions to other people?

1 Chronicles 17:1-15—David's Good Intentions

Let's look at David's response to God's promise of a lasting dynasty for David's family and the great, honored privilege of building the temple. God responds to David's *intentions* rather than to his *accomplishments*. We can ask several questions with relevance to our own lives.

How does God respond to you? To your accomplishments? To your good intentions? What experiences have you had with God that are similar to David's experiences? When conscious of failure, do you find comfort in Paul's stress on the intention of the heart rather than on the achievements of life (see Romans 2:15-16)?

1 Chronicles 21—David's Intercession

In 21:17 David intercedes before God on behalf of the people. David asks God to punish, not the people, but David himself. Many of us, too, use intercessory prayer from time to time. How is intercession a form of looking forward to something better for those for whom we pray?

We do not look for thrones and temples for our children, do we? But what valuable "possession" do we desire for them: A world at peace? A life of reasonable prosperity? Success in family life, in chosen fields of work, and in growth and development as believers in Christ and as members of the church?

In our further reading (1 Chronicles 22:2-5) we shall observe that David, knowing he himself is not to see the temple built, nevertheless provides "materials in great quantity" for the work Solomon will do. What materials may we endeavor to provide for the success of those who will come after us?

The house of the LORD God is to be here. (22:1)

THE TEMPLE AND ITS RITUALS

1 Chronicles 22–29

DIMENSION ONE: WHAT DOES THE BIBLE SAY?

Answer these questions by reading 1 Chronicles 22

1. What materials are gathered for Solomon's later use? (22:2-5)

2. Why is David forbidden to build a temple? (22:8)

3. What will guarantee Solomon's success? (22:13)

Answer these questions by reading 1 Chronicles 23

4. How many adult Levites are counted? (23:3)

5. Why do the Levites no longer need to carry the tabernacle? (23:25-26)

THE TEMPLE AND ITS RITUALS

6. What new duties are assigned the Levites? (23:28-32)

Answer these questions by reading 1 Chronicles 25

7. What temple role is assigned to the sons of Asaph, Heman, and Jeduthun? (25:1)

8. How do Jeduthun's sons prophesy? (25:3)

Answer this question by reading 1 Chronicles 26

9. Why do David and others make dedicated gifts? (26:27)

Answer these questions by reading 1 Chronicles 27

10. What kinds of property does the king have? (27:25-31)

11. What does David's uncle, Jonathan, do? (27:32)

Answer these questions by reading 1 Chronicles 28

12. How does David describe the temple he wants to build? (28:2)

13. How does David become king of Israel? (28:4)

14. Why is Solomon to be king after David? (28:5-6)

15. What advice does David give Solomon? (28:9)

16. Who has written down the plan for the temple? (28:19)

17. Who will help Solomon build the temple? (28:20-21)

Answer these questions by reading 1 Chronicles 29

18. What do the people give to build the temple? (29:7-8)

19. How are these gifts for the temple given? (29:9)

20. What does David say is the Lord's? (29:11)

21. Where do the gifts the men and women offer God come from? (29:14-16)

22. Who is responsible for Solomon's reputation and great splendor? (29:25)

23. How is David's life summarized? (29:28)

DIMENSION TWO: WHAT DOES THE BIBLE MEAN?

Someone has said that the words "study the scriptures diligently" (John 5:39) have undone the world. Originally, the word *undone* meant that the world had been ruined. We, however, are convinced that in the proper understanding of Scripture lies the hope for a world constantly threatened by human ignorance, fear, and sin. That old world will indeed be undone when we hear and respond to the living truth to which Scripture points.

The new world that will be born will be rewarding beyond our fondest dreams. Not just in eternity has God prepared great things for those who love the Lord. When Jesus said his purpose was the bringing of life abundant, his reference was not exclusively to what we expect to discover beyond the grave (see John 10:10)!

What insights might we learn from today's chapters? Consider these:

1. Like David, people of faith will work for realization of promises they cannot expect to see fulfilled.

2. Like David, we need to point our children to paths of fullest obedience to the Lord our God.

3. Like those who joined with David in providing for the temple, we need to bring the best we have to the service of God. We need to bring the gifts of materials and of self with joyful and willing hearts.

■ **1 Chronicles 22.** David—who has been forbidden to build the temple himself—makes material and, to the best of his ability, spiritual and moral preparations for the house of God. His material preparations are vast, costly, and exotic. He has paid an enormous price of "six hundred shekels of gold" for the building site (1 Chronicles 21:25). That is just the beginning of his provisions (see 1 Chronicles 22:14).

But something has to be added if the temple construction is to succeed. That "something else" is the character and conduct of Solomon, who will succeed David. Thus David prays for and advises his son (see 1 Chronicles 22:6-16).

■ **1 Chronicles 23–27.** This large part of the Scripture assigned for today's reading need not attract a major part of our attention. We can get a general idea of the historical content of these chapters by noting headings such as these:

Chapter 23—the order and functions of the Levites. Verses 28-32 suggest the spirit of worship in which we as Christians might share.

Chapter 24—the classification of the priests.

Chapter 25—provisions for those who make the temple services joyful with the sounds of instrumental and vocal music (see esp. vv. 3-7).

Chapter 26—the assignment of duties to the keepers of the temple gates (see esp. vv. 1, 26-29).

Together, these chapters, in which duties are spelled out, paint a glorious picture of the nature of the worship intended to be offered to God in the temple that David envisions and Solomon builds.

Chapter 27—a record of early civil and military organization.

■ **1 Chronicles 29.** Two emphases should be noted in this chapter: (1) the emphasis upon the spirit in which the gifts are given (29:3, 9), and (2) the emphasis upon God as the ultimate giver of all gifts that we enjoy for ourselves. We return a portion of these gifts to God for the wide-ranging ministries of the church upon the earth. David's prayer is appropriate for our concerns for Christian stewardship (1 Chronicles 29:18). We may be reminded of Paul's comments upon the proper spirit in Christian giving (2 Corinthians 9:6-9).

DIMENSION THREE: WHAT DOES THE BIBLE MEAN TO ME?

1 Chronicles 22—Preparing to Build the Temple

David's preparations for the construction of the temple are twofold: by accumulating materials and by advising Solomon on how to proceed. Which is the more urgent of David's attempts to guarantee the success of the temple construction program?

THE TEMPLE AND ITS RITUALS

It is obviously important that such vast quantities of valuable material be available to Solomon. However, what happens if some vital spark is lacking in Solomon himself? What happens to the dream of any generation if those who come after do not have the will, energy, and purpose to share in its fulfillment? How have you carried on the work dreamed by the generation before you? What dreams do you hope will come to fruition in future generations? How are you working to prepare the next generation to fulfill the dreams you have?

1 Chronicles 23:1-6—Administration as Service

In these verses, we see David acting as an administrator. Administration is the arrangement for orderly and efficient conduct of persons. Administration of the *spiritual* and the *secular* business of a people is a gift of God. It is a concern of God as it is a concern of ours. In the New Testament, *administration* is a gift and assignment given by God (1 Corinthians 12:28). It is a kind of service to God.

We must not discount the services of those who do "the pick and shovel work" of the church. The usher has a role as surely as the soloist. The financial secretary for the congregation serves God no less than the Sunday school teacher. All persons, in their own ways, serve to advance the cause of Christ as surely as the person who stands in the pulpit.

These verses also show us the importance of different kinds of service. For David and those who labor with him, there is a fourfold division of responsibility: priests, Levites, musicians, and gatekeepers.

For the New Testament church and for our church today, there is a threefold division of service. First, there is the ministry of sharing insight into the gospel. These persons are variously described as apostles, prophets, and teachers (see 1 Corinthians 12:28). Second, there is the ministry of aid to human needs. These persons we might call social workers. Among the people called Methodists, this includes missionaries and deaconesses, whose calling is to be full of good works. Administration, as noted above, is a third category of service within the body of Christ.

What is your role within the body of Christ? Are you a proclaimer of the gospel? A social worker? An administrator? How can we all share in the one common calling to live our lives responsibly before God and responsively to the needs of humanity?

1 Chronicles 29:6-9—The Spirit of Cooperation

Certain psychological qualities are of the highest moral and spiritual value: unity, cheerfulness, cooperation, and willingness. Wherever these qualities exist—in a marriage, in a family, in a business organization, in a Sunday school class, in a small group, in a congregation—life becomes better for all concerned.

Notice the number of times in this chapter that recognition is made of the willing spirit with which the people give (see vv. 5, 6, 9, 14, and 17). The spirit in which we approach the varied tasks, responsibilities, and opportunities of life is crucial!

Is yours a group that can be counted on whenever there is a task to be done? What roles of service and leadership in your church are played by group members? How many sing in the choir; usher; lead groups; share in special activities for men, women, youth, or children; teach vacation Bible school; assist in building maintenance; participate in a work area of the church; give leadership or service in a community activity that is not specifically church related or church sponsored?

Solomon son of David established himself firmly over his kingdom. (1:1)

10

THE REIGN OF SOLOMON
2 Chronicles 1–9

DIMENSION ONE: WHAT DOES THE BIBLE SAY?

Answer these questions by reading 2 Chronicles 1

1. Where do Solomon and the assembly go to worship the Lord? (1:3)

2. What important artifacts of the faith are at Gibeon? (1:3, 6)

3. What gifts does Solomon ask from God? (1:10)

4. Why does Solomon want these gifts? (1:10)

5. What does God add to these gifts? (1:12)

Answer these questions by reading 2 Chronicles 2

6. Why is the temple to be so great? (2:5)

7. What does Solomon see as the purpose of the temple? (2:6)

8. What aid is the king of Tyre asked to give Solomon? (2:7-10)

9. What is the name of the king of Tyre who helps Solomon? (2:11-12)

10. How will Solomon pay for this assistance by Hiram? (2:15)

Answer this question by reading 2 Chronicles 3

11. What is put in the Most Holy Place of the temple? (3:10)

Answer these questions by reading 2 Chronicles 5

12. What artifacts of the faith are brought to the completed temple? (5:5)

13. Where is the ark placed in the temple? (5:7-8)

14. What is in the ark? (5:10)

THE REIGN OF SOLOMON

15. What are the duties of the trumpeters and the singers? (5:13)

16. When the ark is installed, what sign of God's presence is given? (5:14)

Answer these questions by reading 2 Chronicles 6

17. In what city will God's Name dwell? (6:6)

18. What promise does God keep with the people? (6:14)

19. Can the house that Solomon builds contain God? (6:18)

Answer these questions by reading 2 Chronicles 7

20. What actions will bring forgiveness and healing to the land? (7:14)

21. What will happen if king and people are unfaithful to God? (7:19-20)

Answer this question by reading 2 Chronicles 8

22. How long does it take Solomon to build the temple and his palace? (8:1)

Answer these questions by reading 2 Chronicles 9

23. For what purpose does the queen of Sheba think God has set Solomon over Israel? (9:8)

24. What are the evidences of prosperity in King Solomon's day? (9:27)

25. How long does Solomon reign in Jerusalem over Israel? (9:30)

DIMENSION TWO: WHAT DOES THE BIBLE MEAN?

First Chronicles ends with the death of David. What he had known from the beginning has now come to pass. Solomon is king. The era is at hand when the Lord will permit the building of a house. The succession of David's family, in the person of Solomon, is assured. The people and their leaders have twice declared Solomon to be the rightful successor to his father, David (see 1 Kings 2:12; 1 Chronicles 29:23).

These first nine chapters of Second Chronicles cover Solomon's prayer for wisdom and knowledge (1:8-10), the building and furnishing of the temple (3:1-5:1), the great service of dedication and Solomon's high priestly prayer (5:2–6:42), and God's response to the gift of the house and the repeated injunction that the people must be faithful in their devotion to the one true and living God (7:1-3). The section closes with a "treasurer's report" of the wealth and splendor of Solomon (chs. 8–9).

■ **2 Chronicles 1:7-12.** Solomon has great interest in material possessions, power, and prestige. He has a more-than-healthy dose of the normal human desire to have and to possess. But here at least, Solomon shows an awareness that it is more important to *be* than to *have*. His twofold request for God's gift is more a prayer for character than for possessions, more of a request for quality than for quantity, and more of a request for being than for having.

What is the difference between wisdom and knowledge? For Solomon's task of ruling—and his ambition to rule well—knowledge without wisdom would be a disaster. *Knowledge* is a mastery of facts, and *wisdom* is skill in the application of those facts.

■ **2 Chronicles 6:1-42.** This "high priestly" prayer of Solomon is virtually identical to 1 Kings 8:12-52.

As great as the temple is, Solomon knows that God is not contained there. The temple is to be a focal point where the prayer of the king and subsequent prayers of the people will focus. But God will hear from beyond the temple. From beyond the temple Solomon invokes the healing, forgiving, and renewing grace of God upon the people—God's people and Solomon's people.

Solomon brings a multitude of concerns before God. For each of these concerns, God's response of aid is requested. These include fidelity in agreements between citizens (vv. 24-25), recovery from disaster in times of planting and harvesting (vv. 26-31), the place of the foreigner in Israel (vv. 32-33), victory for Israel in time of war (vv. 34-35), and forgiveness of the sins of the people against God (vv. 36-39).

We often hear that there is no matter of concern to us that we cannot take to God in prayer. Certainly, we see this same attitude reflected in the present passage. Solomon feels free to bring before God any deeply felt concern.

Since there is no God like the God of Israel, characterized by fidelity to the covenant and steadfast love to the people, no anxiety, fear, or need of the people can be alien to God (see 2 Chronicles 6:14). Perhaps Solomon is here anticipating what the Book of Hebrews affirms as the way to approach God in time of need. We believe we can come to God because Christ, our great High Priest, knows our weaknesses.

■ **2 Chronicles 7:1-22.** Fire comes down from heaven, and the offerings are consumed. The glory of the Lord fills the house. These events are tangible evidence of the relationship between God and this chosen people, chosen city, and chosen house of prayer.

But as always, a moral consequence is expected of this special relationship between God and this people. Verses 11-22 set forth three facets of this special moral consequence. First, God's ultimate will and purpose is not punishment and destruction. God intends return, renewal, and healing of the people (v. 14). Second, a special responsibility exists for the ruler of the land. In this case Solomon, son of David, is enjoined to conduct himself as David did (vv. 17-18).

Third, the people and the king must remain faithful to the statutes and commandments of God lest disaster fall upon them; lest exile be their lot; and lest they become an occasion for bitter, ridiculing laughter (vv. 19-22). Is this not precisely the process of ultimate decay and fall that sets in immediately after the death of Solomon?

DIMENSION THREE: WHAT DOES THE BIBLE MEAN TO ME?

2 Chronicles 1:7-12—Knowledge and Wisdom

In this passage, God appears to Solomon and says, "Ask for whatever you want me to give you" (v. 7). Solomon responds by asking for two things: "wisdom and knowledge" (v. 10). Do you pray for more wisdom or for more knowledge, or both? Of what value is knowledge without wisdom or of wisdom without knowledge?

THE REIGN OF SOLOMON

How can we measure the amount of wisdom needed to deal with the complex, perplexing, and changing social order in which we live and in which those who come after us must live?

2 Chronicles 6—The Scope of Prayer

God's concern corresponds to human needs. We can rightfully ask whether there is any need that is improper to bring before God.

What needs to be the scope of our prayers as we pray for our country? We have seen that Solomon feels free to range over a broad spectrum of possible concerns. Can we pray about politics and economics? Labor versus management strife? The persistent evidences of racism in our land? The ominous clouds of war that loom in places around our world?

How are prayers for family, friends, church, and community related to prayers for the well-being of the nation?

2 Chronicles 7—Moral Expectations

As we discussed in Dimension Two, there is always a moral consequence in our relationship to God. That this moral dimension was also part of the relationship between God and the chosen people is clear in this passage from Second Chronicles.

If moral expectancy was God's ultimate relationship to these long-ago persons, is it the same with us today? What morality does God expect of us? What are the statutes and commandments to which Christians might be expected to adhere?

What share do have we in David? (10:16)

11

THE KINGDOM IS DIVIDED
2 Chronicles 10–16

DIMENSION ONE: WHAT DOES THE BIBLE SAY?

Answer these questions by reading 2 Chronicles 10

1. Who succeeds Solomon as ruler of the United Kingdom? (10:1)

2. In what city does Rehoboam have his encounter with Jeroboam? (10:1-3)

3. What bad advice does Rehoboam follow? (10:10-11)

4. Why does Rehoboam reject the elders' advice? (10:15)

Answer these questions by reading 2 Chronicles 11

5. What tribe joins Judah in remaining faithful to the house of David? (11:1)

THE KINGDOM IS DIVIDED

6. Why does Rehoboam not attack Israel under King Jeroboam? (11:4)

7. How does Rehoboam fortify the territory of Judah? (11:5)

8. Why do the priests and Levites of Israel come to Judah? (11:14-15)

9. How do the immigrants aid Judah and Rehoboam? (11:17)

Answer these questions by reading 2 Chronicles 12

10. What evil does Rehoboam commit? (12:1)

11. What king invades the city of Jerusalem? (12:2)

12. How long does Rehoboam reign in Jerusalem? (12:13)

Answer these questions by reading 2 Chronicles 13

13. How long does Abijah, Rehoboam's son, reign in Jerusalem? (13:1-2)

14. Who wins the war between Abijah and Jeroboam? (13:15)

15. Who gives the victory to Abijah and Judah? (13:15)

Answer these questions by reading 2 Chronicles 14

16. When Asa succeeds Abijah, what kind of king does he prove to be? (14:1-2)

17. What steps does Asa take to rid Judah of pagan religious practices? (14:3-5)

18. Who defeats the Cushites when they attack Asa and Judah? (14:12)

Answer these questions by reading 2 Chronicles 15

19. How does Azariah encourage Asa in his reforming efforts? (15:6-8)

20. How does Asa rebuke his grandmother's pagan religious practices? (15:16)

Answer these questions by reading 2 Chronicles 16

21. With what foreign king does Asa ally against Baasha, king of Israel? (16:2-3)

22. How is this dependence on foreign kings received? (16:7-9)

THE KINGDOM IS DIVIDED

23. What is Asa's last mistake? (16:12)

24. How long does Asa reign over Judah? (16:13)

DIMENSION TWO: WHAT DOES THE BIBLE MEAN?

King Solomon, in all his personal glory, goes the way of all flesh. That solemn biblical phrase for death is repeated here: "Then he rested with his ancestors" (see 2 Chronicles 9:31).

Something else occurs, both very human and tragic at the same time. Solomon's successor, Rehoboam, proves not to have the wisdom and knowledge for governing the people that his father had. The young man cannot recognize good advice when it is given. He speaks harshly to his petitioning people; threatens them with heavier burdens of taxation and labor than they carried during the years of Solomon; and as a result, loses the loyalty of all the nation except the tribe of Judah (2 Chronicles 10). We have read this story before when we examined 1 Kings 12:1-19.

The current chapters of study take us through the reign of the first three kings of Judah: Rehoboam (937–920 BC), Abijah (920–917 BC), and Asa (917–876 BC). We cover a period of sixty-one years. An earlier account of Abijah's reign is found in 1 Kings 15:1-8. The reign of Asa is recorded in 1 Kings 15:9-24.

■ **2 Chronicles 10–11.** The Chronicler makes much of the splendor of the temple and the palace and the willing spirit in which the people support Solomon in this extravagant building program. We may wonder, however, if there was not a great deal of dissatisfaction among the people of the land. What are the elements of "harsh labor" and heavy "yoke" that the people complain about (see 2 Chronicles 10:4, 9)?

Forced labor is a major item (see 2 Chronicles 2:2, 17-18). Taxation is a second element in the heavy burden Solomon places upon Israel. Imagine the labor involved in producing the foods required by the royal entourage! What was the source of the enormous amount of gold—666 talents (about 25 tons)!—that came to the king annually (see 2 Chronicles 9:13)? The bills begin to come due.

Military service is another major element (see 2 Chronicles 8:9-10). All this extravagance is extremely costly and, like all money spent for governmental programs anywhere, comes from the labors of the working people of the nation.

Small wonder that the first request addressed to Rehoboam is, in spirit if not in words, akin to what many persons feel today. We need relief from the cost of governmental programs. Rehoboam's foolish response costs him the major part of the kingdom inherited from Solomon, his father, and from David, his grandfather.

Following the rebellion, Rehoboam wants to bring the people together again by military force. He is warned that his effort is against the nature of God, so he settles down to build in Judah (2 Chronicles 11:1-12). He is joined by many refugees from the revival of paganism taking place in Israel under Jeroboam. Second Chronicles 11:15 suggests the depths of the idolatry to which Jeroboam turns.

As his successor, Rehoboam appoints the son of the woman he loves above the other eighteen who are his wives and the sixty who are his concubines (see 2 Chronicles 11:22).

■ **2 Chronicles 12–13.** Tragedy enters, as seemingly secure Rehoboam "and all Israel with him abandoned the law of the LORD" (2 Chronicles 12:1). Jerusalem is invaded by the king of Egypt, and Rehoboam is forced to use brass for his commanders' shields, where his father once used gold (12:9-11).

Disintegration continues as Abijah, successor to Rehoboam in Judah, and Jeroboam, who led the rebellion in Israel, engage in war.

THE KINGDOM IS DIVIDED

The Chronicler affirms that God gave the kingdom to David and his sons "by a covenant of salt" (13:5; "a solemn promise" in the CEV; "unbreakable covenant" in the CEB). The use of salt in offerings to God connotes respect, mutual trust, and commitment to support. Abijah is claiming that attitude to be the nature of the covenant with which God put David upon the throne.

God is repeatedly described as one who keeps the covenant. Whatever the infidelities of the other party in the agreement, God remains true!

Abijah's claim that God is aiding in his struggle is based upon the covenant that God made with the house of David, Judah's maintenance of the true priesthood for the worship of God (13:10), and the true and proper worship of God (13:11). His further assurance of God's aid in the struggle is the faithlessness of Israel (13:8, 11). In the face of Abijah's argument, to fight against Judah is to fight against God (13:12).

Victory does come to Abijah (see 2 Chronicles 13:13-22). But death comes to him as well; and we turn now to Asa, a king who did what was good and right in the eyes of the Lord (14:2).

■ **2 Chronicles 14–16.** In Asa, we find a king who is zealous for the cause of God. He continues the struggle to make Judah's worship of God pure (14:3-4). His heart is blameless in devotion to God. For the Chronicler, the consequence of Asa's attitude is peace, military victories, and prosperity (14:1, 7, 12).

Second Chronicles 15:15 reminds us of the various summaries of times of well-being in the life of the New Testament church (see, e.g., Acts 9:31). We will examine this verse more closely in the Dimension Three portion of this lesson.

DIMENSION THREE: WHAT DOES THE BIBLE MEAN TO ME?

We may read these chapters as "straight history"; this event happened in this way at this time. Or we may read these chapters for what they tell us about the course of a nation's response to the call of God. And we may read these chapters for what they say to us about an individual's response to God.

2 Chronicles 10:12-19—Chaos in the Land

The external circumstances in which nations and individuals live as God's people are always changing. So it was with these ancient people. Good kings and bad, prosperity and material decline, military victory and military defeat, power and helplessness; persons never knew from day to day what to expect.

How are our present circumstances similar to those described in these verses? How are they different? What elements in our lives today are constantly changing? What elements remain the same?

2 Chronicles 13:1-7—A Covenant of Salt

God has not always given us precisely what we ask for. God has not permitted us always to be the final judges of what we should or should not have. In what way has God made a "covenant of salt" with you? In what way has God seemed to be untrue to you? How has God seemed to let you down?

We have seen the basis of Abijah's claim to the favor of God. On what basis may we assume that God's favor is upon us? Is God's favor the result of something we do or of something that God is? When we are, to the best of our understanding and abilities, true and faithful to the

THE KINGDOM IS DIVIDED

knowledge of God we have been given, can we expect God's presence to be among us as a blessing and a gift?

2 Chronicles 14:1-8—God's Work in the World

Some will remember the words of the old gospel song, "Dare to be a Daniel . . . dare to stand alone." Could we not also sing, "Dare to be an Asa"? This passage describes Asa as a person who did what was right in the eyes of God. If we were like Asa, what manner of men and women would we be? Perfect? Imperfect in performance, faultless in intention? Lazy and indifferent? Vigorous and concerned?

Sometimes, a denomination or congregation has been described as "Christianity with its sleeves rolled up"; that is, Christians at work doing the work of God in the world. To what extent is that phrase descriptive of your group? Of your church? In what ways are you a Christian with your sleeves rolled up?

All Judah brought gifts to Jehoshaphat, so that he had great wealth and honor. (17:5)

12

JUDAH'S KINGS
2 Chronicles 17–26

DIMENSION ONE: WHAT DOES THE BIBLE SAY?

Answer these questions by reading 2 Chronicles 17

1. What are the virtues of Jehoshaphat who succeeds Asa as king over Judah? (17:3-6)

2. What kind of teaching mission to Judah does Jehoshaphat sponsor? (17:7-9)

3. What peoples bring tribute to Jehoshaphat? (17:11)

Answer these questions by reading 2 Chronicles 18

4. With whom does Jehoshaphat make a marriage alliance? (18:1)

5. What does Micaiah say that God has done? (18:22)

JUDAH'S KINGS

6. Jehoshaphat escapes at the battle of Ramoth Gilead, but what happens to King Ahab? (18:28-34)

Answer these questions by reading 2 Chronicles 19

7. How does Jehoshaphat do the work of an evangelist? (19:4)

8. Why are the judges appointed by Jehoshaphat to be careful in their work? (19:7)

Answer these questions by reading 2 Chronicles 20

9. Whom does Jehoshaphat trust when he does not know how to defend Judah? (20:12)

10. What is the Chronicler's assessment of Jehoshaphat as king and as a person? (20:32)

11. Is everything in the reign of Jehoshaphat precisely as God wishes it to be? (20:33)

Answer these questions by reading 2 Chronicles 21

12. What does Jehoram do when he comes to the throne? (21:4)

13. With what words does the Chronicler record the death of Jehoram? (21:20)

Answer these questions by reading 2 Chronicles 22

14. Who is Jehoram's successor? (22:1)

15. Who counsels Ahaziah in doing evil? (22:3)

16. Who seizes the throne after the death of Ahaziah? (22:10-12)

Answer these questions by reading 2 Chronicles 23

17. Who leads the rebellion against the queen? (23:1)

18. What rightful heir to the throne does this rebellion establish? (23:3; 24:1)

19. What is the covenant that Jehoiada makes between the people and the king? (23:16)

Answer this question by reading 2 Chronicles 24

20. What happens to Jehoiada's reforms after his death? (24:17-18)

Answer this question by reading 2 Chronicles 25

21. What does Amaziah, son of Joash, do when he comes to the throne? (25:3-4)

JUDAH'S KINGS

Answer these questions by reading 2 Chronicles 26

22. How long does Uzziah reign over Judah? (26:3)

23. From what illness does Uzziah suffer as punishment for his pride? (26:21)

DIMENSION TWO: WHAT DOES THE BIBLE MEAN?

With few exceptions, all the events and persons mentioned in today's chapters are related to the Southern Kingdom, Judah. Judah remained loyal to the house of David when Rehoboam came to the throne after the death of Solomon (see 2 Chronicles 10).

The time period covered in 2 Chronicles 17–26 is 873–742 BC. This one hundred thirty-year period begins with the ascension of Jehoshaphat to the throne and ends with the death of Uzziah. Most of us remember this latter event by the words of Isaiah 6:1: "In the year that King Uzziah died, I saw the Lord, high and exalted, seated on a throne; and the train of his robe filled the temple."

As with almost any historical period, many unfortunate events transpire during this time. We shake our heads in dismay at Jehoshaphat's establishment of a marriage alliance with Ahab in Israel (2 Chronicles 18). We are disgusted by the idea of prophets, presumably spokespersons for God, telling the king of Israel only what they know he wants to hear (see 2 Chronicles 18:4-27). We shudder at the spectacle of a mother who counsels her son in doing wickedness (2 Chronicles 22:3). Murder, family strife, greed—the whole gamut of human failure—are portrayed in these chapters.

From our perspective, reading this history many centuries after the events, we know that moral, spiritual, political, and economic decay has set in. We know that both of the kingdoms—Judah in the south and Israel in the north—are on their way out. Final defeat is only a century or so away. It will come for Judah in 587 BC. Israel will last only until about 721 BC.

While we may learn from observation of sin and failure, let us turn to bright, hopeful spots in our biblical account. We will focus upon the work of King Jehoshaphat, Judah's teaching king, who reigned 873–849 BC (2 Chronicles 20:31), and on the work of Jehoiada, the political priest who restores the throne to the rightful heir, Joash, who reigned 842–800 BC. Between 849 and 842 BC. there was a usurper in control: Queen Athaliah (2 Chronicles 22:10-12). We will also focus on the reign of Uzziah, who gives Judah a long era of peace and prosperity until his death in 742 BC.

■ **2 Chronicles 17–19.** Second Chronicles 17:7-9 and 19:4-11 provide the biblical basis for our designation of Jehoshaphat as "the teaching king." We must remember that the nation is still a theocracy, that is, a nation that perceives itself to be under the direct rule of God. Persons are only God's intermediaries. The real authority over the land and the people is God.

Thus, when the princes, the priests, and the Levites are sent through all the cities of Judah, it is much more than what we might call a religious revival or evangelistic mission. It is a valiant attempt to call a nation to rediscover its roots and to ground itself again in a firm understanding of the original impetus for its existence. Similar efforts are described in Ezra 7:25, 2 Kings 22–23, and 2 Chronicles 34–35. The message seems to be that there is a great potential for reform in national life when the rulers and the ruled come again to sit under the teaching of the law of God.

What was this Book of the Law of the Lord? Scholars have not done as much research into identification of this book as with the recovered book mentioned in 2 Kings 22–23 and 2 Chronicles 34–35 during Josiah's reign. Thus, we cannot easily speak of the book's content. But because the princes, priests, and Levites have this book, something happens to the quality of Judah's life. That renewal and vitalization is reflected in 2 Chronicles 17:10-13: peace, prosperity, and international esteem.

Second Chronicles 19:4-11 again shows the wisdom and ability of Jehoshaphat as a godly leader of his people. Jehoshaphat provides that basic necessity of every secure and hopeful nation: justice without partiality or taking of bribes.

■ **2 Chronicles 23–24.** The Chronicler devoutly believes that God desires direct descendants of David to sit upon the throne of Judah. Athaliah is the granddaughter of Omri (one of several "illegitimate" kings of Israel) and daughter of Ahab, who "did more evil in the eyes of the LORD than any of those before him" (1 Kings 16:30). So when Athaliah seizes the throne, the Chronicler sees this action as a great evil. Athaliah becomes the queen of Judah when Jehoshaphat marries his son to her as an alliance between himself and Ahab (see 2 Chronicles 18:1; 21:1, 6).

Jehoiada the priest! Is he a man of prayer, committed to the worship of God in temple and in home? We may assume so. But now, in a moment of national need, he is also a man of decisive, vigorous action. He becomes the leader of the rebellion to overthrow Athaliah and put Joash on the throne. This rebellion also takes on the nature of a national renewal. As long as Jehoiada lives and influences Joash, the king "did what was right in the eyes of the LORD" (2 Chronicles 24:2). When Jehoiada dies, the reign of Joash changes drastically (see 2 Chronicles 24:17-25).

These chapters describe a moment in a nation's history when direct intervention in political affairs by religious leaders was needed and produced desirable results.

■ **2 Chronicles 26.** Uzziah's fifty-two-year reign is a time of internal security, national expansion, prosperity, and attention to the basic needs of the nation (see esp. v. 10). The Chronicler's assessment of Uzziah is noteworthy: "He did what was right in the eyes of the LORD. . . . As long as he sought the LORD, God gave him success" (2 Chronicles 26:4-5).

As always in human affairs, however, there is a need for caution. Something dangerous lurks within Uzziah. When he grows strong, arrogant pride leads to a serious overstepping of the bounds. He attempts to usurp a role that does not belong to him (26:16-21).

When Azariah the priest stands against this bold aggression, Uzziah becomes angry: "While he was raging at the priests in their presence before the incense altar in the Lord's temple, leprosy broke out on his forehead" (v. 19).

This skin condition was not Hansen's disease against which medical missionaries have worked valiantly in many areas of the world. The term *leprosy* was used in the Old Testament to cover a wide range of skin diseases and fungus growths. Possibly Uzziah's illness is psychosomatic in nature. But the disease, whatever its medical nature, is tragic in its impact. Uzziah dwells alone and is excluded from the house of the Lord (see 2 Chronicles 26:20-21).

DIMENSION THREE: WHAT DOES THE BIBLE MEAN TO ME?

2 Chronicles 17:7-9—Mission in the World

What would the result be of a great, unified teaching mission in which the law of the Lord is studied? How could such a mission bring about the change in human character that must come if violence, crime, injustice, bribery, traffic in narcotics, and materialism are to be overcome?

How can we recover a national self-concept and an understanding of a unified national goal for our country? Have we gone too deeply into the "them-versus-us" mentality to become one nation? Have we gone too far into secularism to become "one nation under God"?

What is the role of each person in this process? For whose allegiance to the law of the Lord are you responsible? For yourself alone, right?

At what point in the nation's life can you, as a single individual, assume responsibility for establishing justice in the land? What is likely to happen to you if you set yourself, alone, to the practice of justice and mercy in all your human relationships?

2 Chronicles 23–24—Church and State

In Dimension Two of this lesson, we referred to Jehoiada as the "political priest." This concept raises the questions: What shall be, or what can be, the relationship between the church and the state in a democratic nation? When have you seen working people, hungry for freedom and literally hungry for bread, taking their faith into the street and to the negotiating table? When have you seen persons, sustained by faith, standing firm for a new measure of freedom and justice in their homeland?

Can something comparable happen to us? What contemporary issues center on the relationship of church and state? Is it possible, for example, that a meeting of minds and a unity of action could take place between pro-abortionists and antiabortionists around a common principle of commitment to the value of human life? What changes in attitudes might be necessary on the part of each? What other issues come to mind? Can you communicate well with persons who hold views different from yours? What problems arise in these situations?

2 Chronicles 26—Pride Leads to Destruction

We have suggested that pride—swelling and growing within Uzziah as his political, military, and monetary power grows—leads to his tragedy. Pride is his point of vulnerability. Pride literally leads to disease in the case of Uzziah.

Is pride your point of vulnerability? From what other secret sins do you need salvation? What are the hidden faults from which you need cleansing? What are the presumptuous sins that seek dominion over you (see Psalm 19:12-13)?

GENESIS to REVELATION **2 CHRONICLES**

Hezekiah had very great riches and honor . . . for God had given him very great riches. (32:27-29)

13

HEZEKIAH AND JOSIAH

2 Chronicles 27–36

DIMENSION ONE: WHAT DOES THE BIBLE SAY?

Answer this question by reading 2 Chronicles 27

1. What is Jotham's attitude toward the temple? (27:2)

Answer these questions by reading 2 Chronicles 28

2. What three sins does Ahaz commit? (28:2-3)

3. What do the Israelites do with their captives? (28:8-11)

4. In his distress, what does King Ahaz do? (28:22)

Answer these questions by reading 2 Chronicles 29

5. What is the Chronicler's assessment of King Hezekiah? (29:2)

HEZEKIAH AND JOSIAH

6. Where did the order for the worship in the temple come from originally? (29:25)

Answer these questions by reading 2 Chronicles 30

7. What great feast does Hezekiah invite Judah and Israel to attend in the restored temple? (30:1)

8. What does Hezekiah promise the people if they will keep the Passover? (30:9)

9. What attitude does Hezekiah regard as being more important than ritual cleanness? (30:18-19)

10. How long has it been since Passover was kept so well in Jerusalem? (30:26)

Answer these questions by reading 2 Chronicles 31

11. Does Hezekiah's revival of religion reach beyond Jerusalem? (31:6)

12. What offerings do the people make? (31:6)

13. What do Hezekiah and the princes do when they see the offerings? (31:8)

14. How does the Chronicler summarize Hezekiah's attitude? (31:21)

Answer these questions by reading 2 Chronicles 32

15. Why does Hezekiah believe Judah can be strong and of good courage against Sennacherib? (32:7)

16. What is the great offense of Sennacherib's servants? (32:19)

17. What is the flaw in Hezekiah's relationship with God? (32:24-5)

Answer these questions by reading 2 Chronicles 33

18. What happens when Manasseh comes to the throne? (33:1-2)

19. What occasions Manasseh's conversion and return to the Lord? (33:11-12)

Answer these questions by reading 2 Chronicles 34

20. How does Josiah bring reform to Judah before he discovers the Book of the Law? (34:3)

21. What great discovery does Hilkiah the priest make? (34:14)

22. What response does Josiah make to the reading of the Book of the Law? (34:31)

HEZEKIAH AND JOSIAH

Answer these questions by reading 2 Chronicles 36

23. What kings after Josiah are taken into exile? (36:4-6, 9-10)

24. On what note of hope does Second Chronicles end? (36:22-23)

DIMENSION TWO: WHAT DOES THE BIBLE MEAN?

These are exciting chapters with which we end our study of many centuries of Hebrew history. We have read about events from the last years of David (who died about 961 BC) to events in the first year of the reign of Cyrus, king of Persia (about 538 BC). The story has been one of rise and fall, of good kings and bad kings, and of faithful and unfaithful people.

Today's chapters cover many significant events. We select these for special study:

1. The amazing act of mercy on the part of Israel toward defeated Judah in the time of Ahaz (28:8-15).

2. The remarkable religious revival that occurs during the reign of Hezekiah (29–32).

3. The reforms under the leadership of King Josiah (34–35).

4. The end of the nation and the beginning of hope (36).

■ **2 Chronicles 28:8-15.** This passage claims our attention as one of those remarkable moments in Hebrew history when someone rejects the common practices of murder, slaughter, and spoil and rises to a great peak of compassion.

This passage sheds light on the oft-repeated and tragically misunderstood statement that the Bible is a progressive revelation of God. That statement does not mean that God is different yesterday, today, and forever. It does mean that, if God is like Christ, then we find many understandings of God, particularly in the Old Testament, that are not complete (see John 14:8-11).

The moral commandments of the Old Testament, which are in harmony with the mind of Christ as described in the Gospels, are binding upon us as Christians. We do not believe that the Old Testament rites, ceremonies, and guidelines for conducting civil affairs are binding upon us. We do find in both the Old Testament and the New Testament an upward call to recognize God's holy, loving, merciful, just, and redeeming nature.

The four sections of our focus for this session illustrate this last element of our understanding of what the Old Testament means for today's Christian disciples. This meaning may be summarized in two parts:

1. God communicates the divine will to those persons who are willing to receive and understand it. In our special study passages, the mind of God is communicated through the written word of God contained in what we know as the Book of Deuteronomy. In one instance, the word is confirmed by a woman prophet, Huldah (2 Chronicles 34:22-28). In another case, it is brought by Oded the prophet to the victorious Israelites, who think at first to destroy or subjugate the people of Judah and Jerusalem (2 Chronicles 28:8-15).

Thus the message of God comes through the written "voice" of Scripture and the living voice of dedicated women and men. That truth is to be found in the contexts of Scripture, tradition, reason, and experience. It is not always easy to arrive at truth in this manner. But what waits at the end is worth the struggle to hear, to understand, and to know.

2. God's ultimate will is discovered in words and messages that come close to harmonizing with the mind of Jesus Christ. As Christians seeking guidance for daily living, we read the Old Testament for the light it sheds on our roots of faith. We rejoice when those roots lead us directly into the mind of Jesus.

HEZEKIAH AND JOSIAH

■ **2 Chronicles 29–32.** In any reading of Hebrew history, the twenty-nine-year reign of Hezekiah has to loom large. Much of the wickedness done by his father, Ahaz, is undone. The temple and its worship are restored. The people of both Israel and Judah are invited to Jerusalem to keep the Passover.

We will look at two passages with special interest. In the first passage (2 Chronicles 30:18-20), we find an anticipation of Jeremiah's great description of the new and inner covenant God desires to establish with the people (see Jeremiah 31:31- 34). Hezekiah does not underestimate the value of ritual cleanliness and so emphasizes the acts of consecration and dedication. But he also stresses that the inner attitude of the person who worships God is of greater importance. Again we think of Jesus: his words to the woman at the well (John 4:23-24), the beatitude for the pure in heart (Matthew 5:8), and his approval of the words of Isaiah (Mark 7:6-8; Isaiah 29:13).

In 2 Chronicles 31:2-19, we read of a program that Hezekiah and the people undertake to bring offerings to Jerusalem. Note two related verses: "He ordered the people . . . to give the portion due the priests and Levites *so they could devote themselves to the Law of the L*ORD" (2 Chronicles 31:4; italics added). Then, of the priests, we read, "they were faithful in consecrating themselves" (2 Chronicles 31:18).

These verses show an important twofold emphasis. First is the responsibility of the people to give. Second is the task to which priests and Levites were set apart: giving themselves to the law of the Lord and keeping themselves holy.

Study of God's Word and purity of personal living: this is the twofold calling of these ancient leaders. Is the calling of religious leaders any different in our own time? Is there a mutual obligation between priest and parishioner, pastor and congregation?

■ **2 Chronicles 34–35.** The reform under King Josiah was founded in a rediscovery of the written law of God, the

Book of the Law, or Book of the Covenant (see 2 Chronicles 34:15, 30).

Prior to this discovery and the great reforms that followed, Josiah had instituted what we might call a "youth-led revival" in his kingdom. At the age of sixteen, he "began to seek the God of his father David"; when he was twenty, "he began to purge Judah and Jerusalem" of pagan practices; and when he was twenty-six, he arranged for the repair of the temple (see 34:3, 8).

We have noted earlier that the Book of the Law comprises a major portion of what we know today as the book of Deuteronomy. What is of great interest is the impact of the written word upon the king and the people. King Josiah repents, consults with the prophetess Huldah for a confirmation of the message, renews the covenant between God and the people, and institutes practical reforms. These activities show the king's desire to lead his people to embrace again the great fundamentals of Israel's original faith.

■ **2 Chronicles 36.** The kingdom comes to an end as three of its kings, in less than twelve years, are taken into captivity and exile (35:1-10). The end comes when the king of the Chaldeans (Babylonians) destroys the temple. Everything and everyone is carried off to Babylon (36:17-20). This final battle occurred about 587 BC, and it was not until 50 years later, about 538 BC, that the exiles began to return home (36:22).

DIMENSION THREE: WHAT DOES THE BIBLE MEAN TO ME?

We read the Old Testament for what it actually is. It is a pre-Christian book. But it is a very special pre-Christian book, for in it we have the foundations for the moral and spiritual faith that is to come to full flower in Jesus and the New Testament church.

HEZEKIAH AND JOSIAH

2 Chronicles 28:8-15—The Limits of Compassion

In this passage, the prophet Oded commands the people to return the captives they have taken in battle with Judah and Jerusalem. Would the Israelites have been able to hear this word of Oded if its message had included peoples beyond the Hebrew community? How wide is the scope of our ability and willingness to forgive and to exercise mercy? Where are our limits?

As we deal with other persons, it is helpful to remember our own faults and failures. What needs do you have that make you more compassionate toward the needs of other persons? What are your faults and failures?

2 Chronicles 30:18-20—God's Covenant

In this passage, Hezekiah stresses that inner attitude is more important than outer ritual. God's covenant is available to those who set their hearts to seek God. What is the ultimate nature of the covenant God has shared with us? Is the covenant given to us through church and Bible as it was channeled to the Hebrews through written word, worship in the temple, and national existence?

What really counts for most of us is the heart-to-heart, mind-to-mind relationship we are permitted to have with God. Romans 8:14-17 speaks of the inner witness of the Holy Spirit. How is such a witness meaningful for you?

2 Chronicles 31:2-19—Clergy and Laity

What responsibility does a congregation have to its pastor and, in turn, what are the special responsibilities of the pastor? Second Chronicles 31:2-19 suggests that the laity have responsibility for material support of the clergy. Few of us would question that. But what is the central calling of the pastor? Is it the same as the responsibility of these priests and Levites, to give self to the law of God and to be holy? Or are the real responsibilities of the pastor to get a lot of new members, to fill the church, to raise the budget, and to be good with the young people? Of course these duties are important. But are they meant to be byproducts and outcomes of God's specific calling of a man or woman to the Christian ministry, or are they the central responsibilities?

In this passage, we find elements of mercy and compassion that remind us of the words of Jesus in Matthew 25:31-46. We might even hear overtones of Luke 10:29-37. In this ancient act, prompted, in part at least, by the Israelites' awareness of their own sin, we come close to the mind that is in Jesus Christ.

2 Chronicles 34–35—Religious Reform

The contrast between the religion of the Hebrew people and the religion of the surrounding nations is the contrast between morality and immorality. The reforms of Josiah also represent a striving for unity among the Hebrew people. The emphasis upon Jerusalem as the one proper place for the true worship of God is a political and national move as well as a spiritual one. It is a means of unifying the people.

Now let us ask if we wish people to become Christians? Do we care if they ever become believers in our Lord? Why is it important that persons become committed Christians?

2 Chronicles 36:17-23—Love or Justice?

The kingdom ends. We are reminded of the twofold role of Jeremiah: (1) to pronounce doom upon the sinful people in the name of a holy God (see Jeremiah 27), and (2) to pronounce eventual restoration and salvation in the name of a loving and mercy-filled God (see Jeremiah 30–31).

The Scripture here and elsewhere suggests that, in the end, love outweighs law, mercy goes beyond justice, and favor reaches across human failure. How does the present passage reflect this suggestion? What evidence do you see in our society that supports this suggestion? How do God's love and God's law balance in your own life?

THE KINGDOMS OF ISRAEL AND JUDAH

About the Writer

Charles R. Britt wrote these lessons on First and Second Kings and First and Second Chronicles. At the time of writing, he was an assistant professor of family and child development at Auburn University, Auburn, Alabama. He was an ordained elder of the Alabama-West Florida Conference of The United Methodist Church.